W9-CJQ-955

CHÂTEAUX OF THE LOIRE

GREAT GALLERIES SERIES

CHÂTEAUX OF THE LOIRE

Text by
GEORGES POISSON
Assistant Keeper of the City of Paris Museums

MEREDITH PRESS · NEW YORK

First published in the United States in 1968
by Meredith Press
Des Moines and New York

Translated from the French
by
James Brockway

Printed in Italy for Meredith Press

to JACQUES LEVRON

Loire, land of châteaux... Look where one will in the world, one will find few regions where these country castles, these ' demeures de plaisance ', built between the 15th and 17th centuries, often to replace military fortresses, occur in such large numbers. By comparison, the castles of the Rhine are no more than a scattering of primitive strongholds, generally fallen into ruin. The Île-de-France châteaux, often so despised, have benn decimated by the expansion of Paris.

But the expression ' the châteaux of the Loire ' does not refer to a precisely defined geographical region. Though these residences are ranged along the banks of the ' queen of rivers ', from Gien—or even, for that matter, from Nevers—to Nantes, they are also dotted along the valleys running parallel to the Loire, through which flow the river's tributaries. It is impossible to leave out Chenonceaux, situated on the Cher, Azay-le-Rideau, erected on the banks of the Indre, Chinon, dominating the Vienne, le Plessis-Bourré, rising up from the Sarthe; impossible to avoid mention of the châteaux far from the rivers: Chambord, with its tiny rivulet, le Cosson, Cheverny, Valençay, Montgeoffroy. So the Val de Loire of the châteaux would be a geographical region corresponding roughly with the ancient provinces of Orleans (together with le Blésois and la Sologne), of Touraine and Anjou, to which could be added the part of Brittany round Nantes. It would be difficult, too, to separate the châteaux of the Orleans area, Gien, La Bussière, from those of Burgundy (Saint-Fargeau) and to distinguish between the residences of Touraine, Le Grand-Pressigny, Montrésor, and the châteaux of Berri (Châteauneuf-sur-Cher), the manor-houses of Anjou, Landifer, Durtal, from the buildings in the Le Mans region (Le Lude). And in the matter of châteaux, who can say where Brittany ends and the Val de Loire begins?

Despairing of ever arriving at a clear geographical definition, some authorities have attempted to define the region on an architectural and chronological basis—reserving the appellation of ' châteaux of the Loire ' for those edifices which date from the Renaissance, even if built very far away from the Loire. This is the course Monsieur François Gébelin, the leading specialist on the matter, has followed. He has gone as far as to include Le Lude, in the Le Mans district, and even Gaillon, in Normandy, in this category, the paradoxical in this approach merely illustrating the difficulty of the problem. If the châteaux of the Loire represent the finest flowering of the Renaissance in France, they are not only that—anymore than the Renaissance can be summed up by reference exclusively to them.

Our purpose has been more modest, more diverse, too. Traversing the region, we have been intent to show the most famous residences, chancing to go as far south as Grand-Pressigny and Azay-le-Ferron, to penetrate into Sologne as far as Moulin, to go north as far as Landifer, and to follow the river as far as Nantes. And while showing exterior views, both old and new, of these celebrated homes, we have also made a point of showing a few of the admirable works of art which adorn their interiors and which are often overlooked owing to the splendour of their architecture. It has also been our purpose to show some of the less famous of these châteaux.

What was the reason for this proliferation? Why so many châteaux in the Loire region, when Champagne, Rousillon, even Provence are so destitute of them? To answer this question it will be necessary to outline the entire history of the châteaux of the Loire... without, however, any guarantee of finding the answer.

This region, seeming from its geography to be dedicated to unity, furrowed as it is by the parallel valleys of the Loire, Cher, Indre, Vienne, all waterways of economic and cultural significance, was recognized early on to be of strategic importance, indeed as early as the time of Clovis, who made Chinon one of the principal fortresses in his kingdom. But from early medieval times it was severely parcelled up—the work of feudalism, which created a mass of small, often rival territories here. From the end of the 10th century on, competing princes—Foulques Nerra, Count of Anjou, Thibaut le Tricheur, Count of Blois, endeavoured to re-unite them and, consequently, to defend them against their neighbours—a matter of protecting conquests all the more fragile for being recent. It was this which gave birth to these keeps, all constructed on the lines of Langeais, possibly the oldest in France. Rectangular, massive, flanked by buttresses, Beaugency,

Montrichard, Montbazon, above all, Loches, built at the end of the 11th or the beginning of the 12th century, these prove today that they were built to resist assault, even the assaults of time.

The Val de Loire of the time was Angevin territory: in the second half of the 12th century the dynasty of Geoffroy Plantagenêt, builder of the first château of Angers, carved out for itself in the Anjou and Touraine region a state—one might even say a kingdom—which challenged the very existence of the Capet dynasty occupying the French throne. After it had established itself on the English throne, the Angevin family still preferred to stay on the banks of the Loire. Henry II lived for most of the time at Chinon, where he had the fort Saint-Georges built and from which point he conducted the struggle against the King of France, who was determined to re-establish his territory's integrity. To begin with, there was the hard war against Louis VII, fought from 1173 and 1177, during the course of which the king's armies appeared several times in Anjou; then, in 1186, the struggle was resumed against a young but by no means unequal adversary, Philippe Auguste (Philip II of France). The battles were fought on the banks of the Loire and in 1189 another keep, that of Villandry, had the distinction of seeing the King of France triumph over Henry II of England and impose his peace terms on him. For the Plantagenets of Anjou this marked the beginning of decline. The aged king, defeated, betrayed by his sons, went to die at Chinon, where Richard Coeur de Lion appeared between two sorties, and where, it is said, they took his body in 1199. Five years later, Philippe Auguste appeared before the fortress, symbol of Angevin dominion, and took it after a siege lasting ten months. In 1206 Anjou and Touraine were finally re-united with the Kingdom of France.

The Age of the Crusades had transformed military architecture here, as it had all over France. The square tower was replaced by the cylindrical keep, less susceptible to damage from artillery fire, although so far that damage was still very modest. It will be found at Montpoupon, Cinq-Mars and Chinon. But, most important of all, walls were added to the simple, primitive tower, ramparts flanked by towers and adapted to the terrain. The earliest example still remaining is Angers, built by St. Louis, the colour of which adds a human touch to its warlike appearance and which has lost the upper section of its towers. Luynes, then known as Maillé, has also retained the same appearance, from the side of the valley, as it had in this epoch. At the same time, the Châtillon family at Blois replaced Thibaut le Tricheur's château by a large fortress, the main remnant of which is the Assembly Room (Salle des Etats).

The 14th century saw Chinon's defences perfected—the Knights Templars were imprisoned there— and new towers added, connected by a whole network of underground tunnels on the outside. War returned to the Loire valley and the English retook Langeais and held it until 1360, while brigands installed themselves in the château of Chenonceaux, from which they were to be expulsed by Du Guesclin. Shortly afterwards that debonair château, Saumur, one of the few châteaux of the duc de Berri to remain intact, was built, and towards the end of the century the main tower at Sully-sur-Loire, probably the work of the great architect Raymond du Temple. A few years later the château was reconstructed by the La Trémoilles.

After 1391 the property at Blois had been bought back from the Counts of Châtillon by Louis d'Orléans, brother of Charles VI. The legend goes that, having conquered the heart of the countess, the duke obtained sums of money from her of such a size that the count was ruined and had to sell him the château. A few years later the handsome duke was assassinated by his cousin, Jean sans Peur, his widow, Valentine de Milan, retiring to Blois, to die there the following year 'of anger and grief.'

At Loches the keep and its two enceintes were flanked by new works, like the Tour ronde, constructed about 1415, making the château a grandiose example of an architecture which, after having served for struggles between local seigneurs, was to become more and more the symbol of the power of the monarch.

Yet of these sovereigns, the first to live on the shores of the Loire, Charles VII, cut a paltry figure. Having fled Paris (surrendered to the Burgundians, on the night of May 28, 1481—he was not to see the city again until twenty years later), he had chosen his residence in the duchies of Berri and Touraine, where he was not even always safe, or respected; insulted during his journey at Azay-le-Rideau, he had the château burned to the ground and its Burgundian garrison massacred.

The man they called 'the king of Bourges' could more properly have been called 'the king of Chinon', for it was between the walls of this fortress, facing the countryside of Vienne, that the 'gentil Dauphin' awaited—with a certain passivity—the crumbling of the last vestiges of his kingdom, of which Orleans was the last bolt. Blois, often threatened, had been saved only by the grace of Dunois, guardian of the possessions of his half-brother, Charles d'Orléans, prisoner of the English. Even Langeais, a few miles from Chinon, had been taken in 1427 and had only been reconquered by the employment of money. The region was not safe and some local noblemen, like the seigneur of Trèves, had new castles built. Charles's army was a mere skeleton of an army and discouraged into the bargain, his coffers were empty, and it was said that the shoemaker at Chinon would not repair his other shoe until the repair of the first had been paid for. The Estates General, gathered together in the château, writhed in their impotence.

On March 8, 1429, a young woman who had arrived from Lorraine was introduced into the grand chamber of the royal apartments, which today has the sky for a ceiling. Ignoring the nobleman seated on the throne, she squeezed a way through the crowd and went up to a gentleman in simple dress, standing apart from the rest. 'A lance's distance away from him, she put one knee to the ground.

'May God grant you long life, gentil Dauphin.'

'You've got the wrong one,' said the man she had addressed, indicating the throne.

'May it please God,' Joan of Arc replied, 'but you are he and none other'.

A moment later the young woman drew the prince aside to a window opening and in a few words, pronounced *sotto voce*, dispelled the doubt which was torturing him: yes, he was, indeed, the dead king's son, legitimate heir to the throne of France.

Charles VII—who can blame him?—would not allow himself to be convinced without more ado and had Joan taken to the du Coudray fort at the château's western extremity, where, during an interrogation lasting several days, the young woman replied to the questions the scholars put to her to their complete satisfaction.

The ground had been prepared for the reconquest. A year later it was at Sully that Joan of Arc decided to drive the English out of France. But times had changed. Charles VII, fallen once again under the unfortunate influence of La Trémoille, was surfeited with success and crossed La Pucelle's plans. Despairing of ever convincing him, Joan left Sully without obtaining the king's leave. She was never to see Charles again.

Tours had been royal since Philippe-Auguste, Angers became royal under Louis XI, Nantes under Charles VIII, Blois and Orléans after Louis XII had ascended the throne. The second half of the 15th century, bringing with it the termination of the Hundred Years' War, marked the arrival of peace in the Val de Loire, while the process of feudal dismemberment slackened off little by little, thanks to the increased authority of the throne. Quite naturally, the châteaux had to lose their military equipment and become country seats. This trend had actually already set in some time before: Joan of Arc had known this royal home at Loches, these 'ancient rooms', with their windows wide open to the skies of Touraine, where she had persuaded Charles VII to go and have himself crowned at Reims, and which remind us less of her, the Saint, than of the lovely Agnès Sorel, whose smile, still to be found on the effigy on her tomb, had perhaps been seen at these sunbathed windows.

Before long the sombre apartments in the keeps were abandoned and domestic quarters built beyond the walls and provided with very slight defences: this is what happened at Montsoreau, at Montreuil-Bellay, at Plessis-lez-Tours, at the château du Moulin. And even where the exterior still retained its military aspect, this merely hid a country house contained within the fortifications, as at Luynes, or more simply, built back to back with the fortifications, as at Boumois or, the prime example, at Langeais, which was built during the second half of the 15th century and seems to be making a display of its power in order not to have to use it. At Ussé, built during the same period, the quadrilateral, flanked by round towers and rather austere to begin with, is made more human in appearance later on. Finally, at Plessis-Bourré, built by the selfsame Jean Bourré who directed the building operations at Langeais, the ramparts were lowered, leaving the seigniorial residence open, its façade pierced by numerous mullion windows letting in the air and the light. The breadth of the moats was relied upon mainly for defence purposes, this limiting artillery fire, while providing the château with a setting to the charm of which men are still susceptible today.

It is, it seems, from this period that the region's fascination dates. Charles VII had gone there of necessity but stayed on by choice. In his twenties he had fallen irrevocably in love with the Val de Loire and only three weeks after his return to Paris, he hastened to return there. He remained there till his death, his nobles and his successors following his example. It must be praised, this region, both for its moderate climate—its summers being freshened, its winters tempered, by the maritime breezes blowing up its valleys—and for its economic stability—an entirely agricultural region, easily able to support an increased population in the form of one or more courts. Far from his country's threatened frontiers, here the king was in the heart of France, in his own domain.

Add to these virtues the easy communications—for at this period the Loire was still navigable; add, too, the Angevin and Tourangel smile, and it becomes simpler to understand why a class of seigneurs should have taken root here, men who were not tardy to profit by the excellent building materials it offered and soon had its masons busy at work. One of the first to be active here was Charles d'Orléans, the gentle poet, returned at last from captivity. For some considerable time it was even believed that it was he who had built the wing at the château of Blois which still bears his name, though it is, in fact, of rather later date: this abode, with its stairway-tower, its promenade, its arcades, its large windows, is already far more of a town mansion than a château, a castle.

During the whole of the 15th century the local seigneurs were busy transforming or reconstructing their homes; the first was Montreuil-Bellay, where all around the old keep other buildings began to grow up, dispersed here and there; then there was Luynes, where a charming residence, which owed much to Plessis-lez-Tours, developed inside the walls. In Anjou the Brézés raised the great towers of Brissac. And if Frances II, Duke of Brittany, gave his château at Nantes an obviously military aspect, this was because it commanded a frontier and one which was beginning to give the kings of France cause for concern. As for King René, the gay and last sovereign of Anjou, he improved his château at Angers and built unpretentious little manor houses all over his territories.

Even Louis XI, who one understands to have been little susceptible to such smiling things as flowers and young girls, and whose rough task of collecting territories kept him busy for twenty years, furrowing away at France in every sense of the word, even he remained eternally attached to this Val de Loire, near to which he was born (Mehun-sur-Yèvre) and brought up (Loches). It was, for that matter, this last-named château which he chose for the installation of his famous wooden cages in which he incarcerated many prisoners of note in the same way as he had poor Cardinal Balue.

At this period, lack of safety on the roads prompted certain local lords to build new homes which it would be easy to defend. Langeais is an example, a château typical of this last flare-up of military architecture. Louis XI himself reinforced the defences of Loches. The king had besides to repress feudal revolts in the region: Pierre d'Amboise, having compromised himself in the League of Public Good, saw his château at Chaumont razed to the ground and, having repented, obtained permission to rebuild it. In doing so, he deliberately chose the cause of peace and security and built a home the uselessness of whose apparent defences was obvious to all. The drawbridge is a triumphal gateway and the walk round the battlements a pleasant promenade. It is a décor to which only the nobleman had the right; one might almost say it is theatrical.

It was to Touraine that the king returned to die. There he had had built a small château of brick at Plessis-lez-Tours, one which hardly matches the picture we have often been given of this monarch. A delightful little residence, decorated, but without fortifications, and surrounded by ravishing gardens crowded with birds where the master gardener, Pierre Benoist, married colour to colour and created orchards. It was here François de Paule, the hermit of Calabria, came to prepare the king, that old warrior, for his final battle.

His successor, Charles VIII, had the same, indeed, even more right to call himself a child of the Val de Loire, and it was from his reign on that the construction of châteaux in this region became, to use M. F. Gébelin's expression, 'the deed of the monarch', a work which proceeded directly from the royal will. Born and raised at Amboise, where he died, he did not wish to quit his home when he ascended the throne and he was soon at work transforming the cheâteau into a royal residence worthy of the name. Guarded by enormous towers which are simply entrance gateways to the 'plate-forme', a grandiose, elongated ring of buildings came to occupy the summit of the hill, accompanied by a graceful chapel which bears signs of the Flemish influence. Nevertheless, it was Langeais he chose for his wedding with Anne de Bretagne, and he went to spend his honeymoon at Plessis-lez-Tours, while his sister, Anne de Beaujeu, 'the least foolish woman in France', celebrated the success of her regency by having the château of Gien rebuilt in an elegant style which employed various shades of brick, the château being open over a broad front and having a tower which was nothing more than an architectural gesture.

It is to the end of the 15th century, too, that it is possible to date back Le Moulin, where the symbolic 'enceinte', designed to run along the 'terre-plein', was never completed, and Talcy, on the frontier of la Beauce, where the massive keep guards a discreet, provincial courtyard and where a graceful gallery opens on to a perspective of other courtyards. In designing this gallery, the architect doubtless took Blois—the Blois of Charles d'Orléans—as his model, as was the case at Fougères-sur-Bièvre and at Beaugency.

But it was Amboise which was to mark the introduction and triumph of the Italianate style. Returning in 1495 from his pointless escapade in Italy, the king brought fifteen ornamental sculptors back with him, among them being Guido Mazzoni, Jérôme Pacherot, Alphonse Damasse and Dominique de Cortone, all of them raised on the art of the Charterhouse at Pavia. Taking over Amboise, they impressed their stamp (still very discreet) there in the keystones of the vault of the tour des Minimes and the tour Hurtault, where various *motifs* belonging to the Gothic tradition appear.

It was in this château at Amboise that the destiny of the monarchy was to be plotted once more. The king, Charles VIII, was amusing himself, awaiting without impatience the birth of an heir who was to receive from him the double crown of France and Brittany. At Blois, the duc d'Orléans, cousin to the king, was holding in check a grumbling opposition.

One day in April 1498, the duke was in the courtyard of the château, surrounded by his followers, when a messanger, covered in dust, arrived from the royal court, leaped off his horse, and knelt before him.

'Sire...'.

All present looked up on hearing this form of address.

'Sire, the king is dead'.

On his way to watch a game of tennis in the drained moat at Amboise, Charles VIII had struck his head violently against a low doorway and within a few hours lay dead. The duc d'Orléans had become Louis XII of France.

Brittany, allied to France by Charles VIII's marriage to Anne de Bretagne, was free again. Political expediency now commanded what human inclination had already hoped for, and Louis XII married Anne... at the price of perjuring himself. Caesar Borgia, a son of the Pope, arrived with great pomp at Chinon, bringing with him the bull annulling Louis's marriage with Jeanne de France. Jeanne the Lame, repudiated, retired to Bourges. Five centuries later, the Church was to make her a saint. It was at Nantes, in the royal apartments with their high, ornamental windows, that Louis XII married Anne of Brittany.

Ten years before these events took place, Louise of Savoy, the Duchess of Angoulême, had taken herself to Plessis-lez-Tours to implore the aid of François de Paule, desperate at her childlessness. The 'good man of Calabria', having reassured the little duchess—who was only 13 years of age—that nothing had been lost, predicted that her son would become king.

The prediction had seemed improbable, the Angoulême family being far removed from the throne. But Louis XII's accession made little François next in line of succession. He and his mother came to live at Chinon, from where they were present at Anne de Bretagne's desperate endeavours to give birth to a dauphin. A divine curse rested upon the royal couple. Eight times the queen had become pregnant at Blois and eight times she had given birth to daughters or to corpses. Desperate, she was obliged to consent at a meeting of the Estates General of Plessis-lez-Tours in 1506 to the marriage of her daughter Claude to the detested heir. Pleased with this decision, before going their several ways, the deputies conferred on the king the title of 'father of the people'.

While arranging the affairs of state at Blois and winding up the Italian venture, Louis found time to please his queen by having the splendid façade at Blois built—one in which he, himself, appears, in the form of an equestrian statue over the entrance, pillars, covered with Anne's emblem, the ermine, supporting the gallery on the first floor. This façade allowed the Italian influence full rein to display a whole repertoire of new-style decorative effects, *motifs* derived from antiquity replacing the flora of the Gothic style, while fully-rounded sculptures succeeded the carved reliefs of the flamboyant period. In the buildings of the succeeding period this form of decoration, widespread at first, was to draw in its frontiers further and further, occurring only in a few, choice sites.

It was on the first floor of this wing that Anne de Bretagne died on January 9, 1514, during a very hard winter. The king, aged, bent, dispirited, looked upon the body of the woman for whom he had perjured himself and said: 'Build a tomb large enough to take both her and me. Before a year has passed, I shall be with her, keeping her company.'

Despite a new marriage, hastily arranged in the desperate hope that even at this late date an heir might be born, Louis's hand had been played out and the crown was to pass to the strapping young fellow waiting impatiently at Chinon. 'Before a year has passed...'.—on January 1, 1515, Louis XII died in his turn.

And so began the great era which was characterized by a flamboyant monarch, François I—a man of far more assured and decided artistic tastes than his predecessors—and by the complete assimilation into French style of all manner of Italian decorative elements. Brick gave way to white tufa-stone and new houses rose, constructed of this admirable material.

At the commencement of the new reign, Thomas Bohier, in charge of the treasury, had Chenonceaux reconstructed, a château planted on the banks of the Cher, with broad vistas over the river and very sumptuous in its interior decoration, of which we still possess, among other things, a timber ceiling bearing the seigneur's monogram. At Réaux, which dates from the same period, the postern, surrounded by tours, makes a triumphal entrance, enlivened by chequerwork in brick and stone. It was from here, perhaps, that this fashion spread to Normandy.

But the principal 'workshop' at the beginning of the new reign is formed by the château of Blois. On both sides of the old ramparts, two wings rose, one of them, on which the Italian profiles of the cornice appear, served primarily as a framework for the splendid staircase—more of a balcony than a staircase—while the other, and more original, was the façade des Loges, which bears witness to Bramante's influence. A small room in one of the apartments, erroneously referred to as Catherine de Médicis' room, still retains its original decoration, consisting of small panels bearing arabesques in sculpture work.

Nevertheless, when at Blois—where he received the Emperor Charles V—François I was not so much at home as at his wife Claude's home. A few years later he decided to create at Chambord a symbol of the power of the throne, as Louis XIV was to do later at Versailles, and for this purpose he chose a medieval plan in which the keep and corner towers do not seem to have any other function than to support the terraced roofs.

A new château on a traditional theme. The resemblance between its lay-out and that of Vincennes has often been remarked upon, and Monsieur Pierre du Colombier has, for his part, drawn attention to the fact that the profusion and decorative effect of the upper structure make the château more like the French châteaux of the 15th century than Italian models. The novelty resided in the great size, the regular distribution of the pillars along the walls, the abundance of Italian *motifs* (niches, vases in the shape of shells), the famous double spiral staircase, sometimes associated with Leonardo da Vinci, and, to an even greater degree, in the classical spirit, evidenced by a certain aloofness and majesty.

Following the king's example, the entire French nobility took to building châteaux in the Val de Loire. Gilles Berthelot raised Azay-le-Rideau, whose corner towers are surmounted by elegant turrets. He profited little by it and François I acquired the château. Jean Le Breton built Villesavin, with its delicately decorated ground floor. It was hardly more than a hunting lodge. Sansac, Le Gué-Péan, Saint-Aignan, l'Islette followed the trend and even provincial residences farther away, like Azay-le-Ferron, were modelled on the royal homes, the local masons being left to interpret the new style in their own fashion, as they have done at Landifer.

Chambord marked both the apogee and the end of the royal presence in the region. Returning from captivity in Madrid in 1526, François I removed his court to Île-de-France. Yet the provinces were never deserted, neither by the king, who returned there many times and, in particular, in 1539 to receive Charles V at Amboise and Chambord, nor by the seigneurs, who continued the sovereigns' architectural activities on their own account. It is at Villandry that, in 1532, we see the towers give way to square pavilions pierced by windows in a less adorned style. Then there is Beauregard, which during Henri II's reign acquires a gallery, decorated a few years later. Valençay, with its two wings at right-angles to each other and its round towers topped by bulbous roofs. Brézé, Herbault, le Grand-Pressigny; Serrant, almost classical in its inspiration. It was Chambord that Henri II chose for signing the treaty by which France re-acquired the three bishoprics of Metz, Toul and Verdun, and he gave Chenonceaux to Diane de Poitiers, who enriched it with ornamental gardens and made it a symbol of her power in so pronounced a fashion that after the king's death Catherine de Médicis took it from her, forcing the favourite to exchange it for Chaumont.

Civil war brought the royal court to the Loire Valley, which was to be torn apart by the religious struggles. In 1560, the court, threatened by the conspiracy led by Condé, took refuge at Amboise, where the conspirators fell, one by one, into the traps which had been prepared for them. François de Guise, the real ruler of the kingdom, had them hanged from the château balcony in the presence of the young king, François II.

Two years later Charles IX, Catherine de Médicis, Henri de Navarre and Condé met at the small château of Talcy, on the banks of the Beauce, seeking to arrive at the agreement they had so far sought in vain. In 1563, Catherine signed a treaty at Amboise granting the Protestants liberty to worship in several cities, but this agreement soon became null and void. The massacre of St. Bartholomew gave the signal for further massacres in the valley, led in the main by the savage seigneur de Montsoreau.

Between two journeys, two attempts at conciliation, Catherine stayed at Chenonceaux and had a gallery built on Philiberth Delorme's bridge across the river, giving sumptuous parties there in honour of Charles IX and later Henri III. In 1577, in honour of the latter monarch, the most beautiful women of the court, all but nude, their hair all dishevelled, organized an unforgettable banquet over which the king presided, clothed in a robe of damask, powdered and *décolleté*, so that in the words of the chronicler: 'everyone wondered whether he was looking at a female king or, perhaps, a male queen'.

After parties of this kind, this same king endeavoured tirelessly to re-establish peace between the Huguenots and the Roman Catholics, and to this end he ordered the château of Angers, among others, to be demolished—an order fortunately countermanded soon afterwards.

The drama reached its height—and conclusion—at Blois, in 1588.

The kingdom of France was in utter disarray. Henri III, clearheaded but at the end of his tether, had been obliged to convoke the Estates General on the banks of the Loire and at its head stood his direst enemy, Henri de Guise. De Guise forced the king to annul his edicts relating to the Protestants, thus re-igniting the civil war, while denying the king the means to bring it to an end. This session, in the great 13th century hall, was one of the most humiliating episodes in the history of the French monarchy. The king, despised by his enemy and his followers, had to suffer the indignity of their sarcasm and their remonstrances, reading in their eyes a prediction of his dethronement. But it did at least show Henri III what he had to do. Two kings of France was one king too many—one of them would have to go. This would be the price of preserving the royal house of Capet.

What happened next is all too well known. Summoned to the château at dawn, on December 23, 1588, apparently for consultations, the duke was wilily separated from his bodyguard and drawn, by a route prepared beforehand, into a perfectly timed trap. On the spot where he was attacked one can still imagine the figure of the Duke, set upon by the Forty-five:

'Gentlemen, what treason is this?'

Shaking off the pack of dogs clinging to his person, Henri de Guise dragged his assailants from one corner of the hall to the other, smearing the walls and curtains with his blood and finally falling to the ground, covered with dagger wounds, at

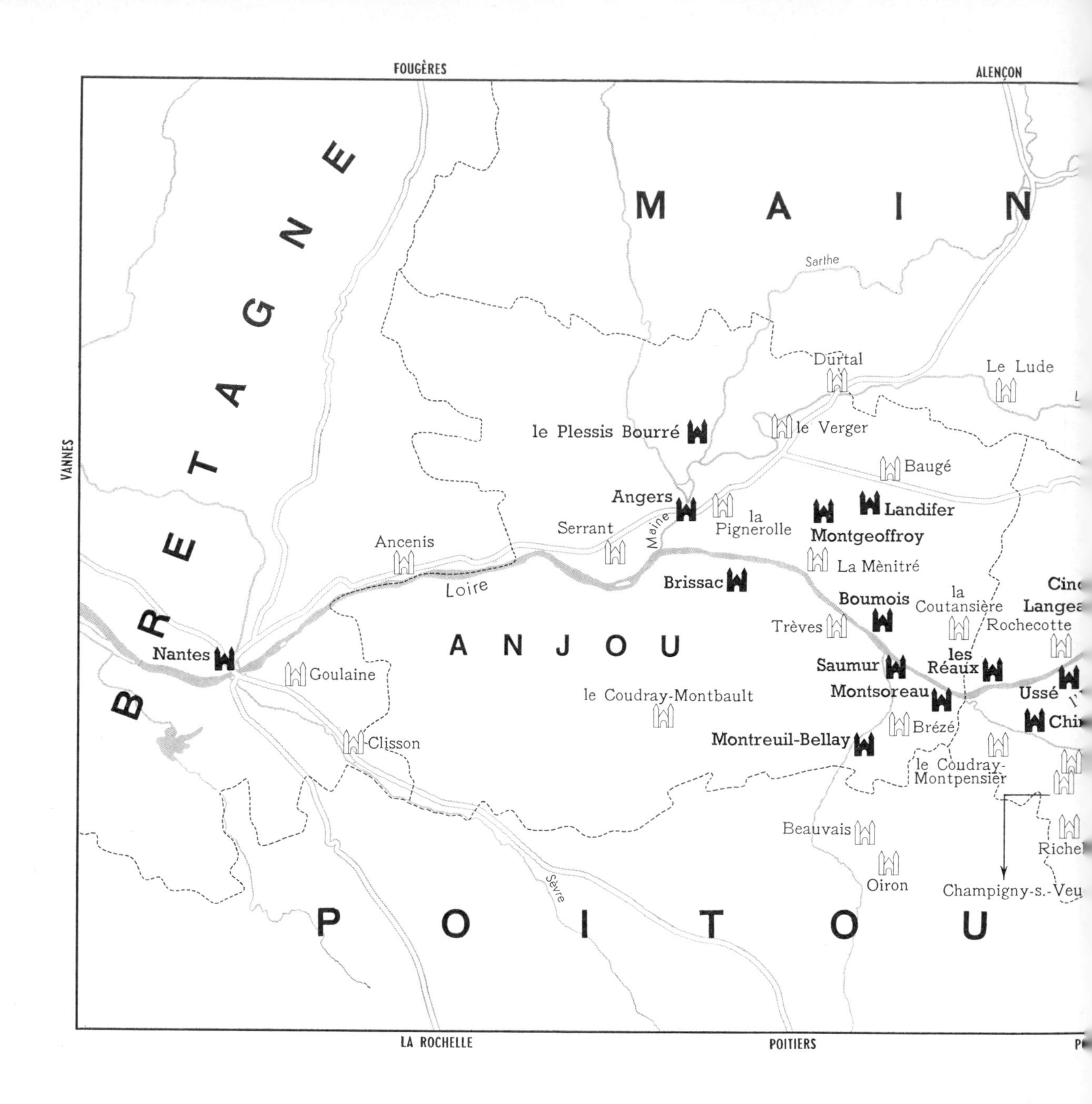

the foot of the king's bed. Livid, tortured, the king arrived at the side of the huge corpse, had the body searched and found in its pocket a note, a terrible justification:

'To keep up the civil war in France will require 500,000 écus a month.'

This death was to be followed by another, even more abject. On Christmas Eve, for the sum of 400 livres, two hardened soldiers agreed to assassinate the Cardinal de Guise, imprisoned under the tiles of the château. He was killed by strokes of the sword, after his velvet, ermine-trimmed robe had been snatched from his body.

A few days later, also at Blois, Catherine de Médicis died during a tempest. It was said by Pierre de l'Estoile that no more notice was taken of this woman, who had previously held the rudder of state with so firm a hand, than if she had been a dead goat.

In the succeeding spring, at Plessis-lez-Tours, Henri III was reconciled with the man who, six months later, was to become Henri IV. After five years of warfare, it was to be given to the new king to put an end to the struggle. On April 13, 1598, he signed the Edict of Nantes, no doubt in the Assembly Room of the château of the dukes of Brittany.

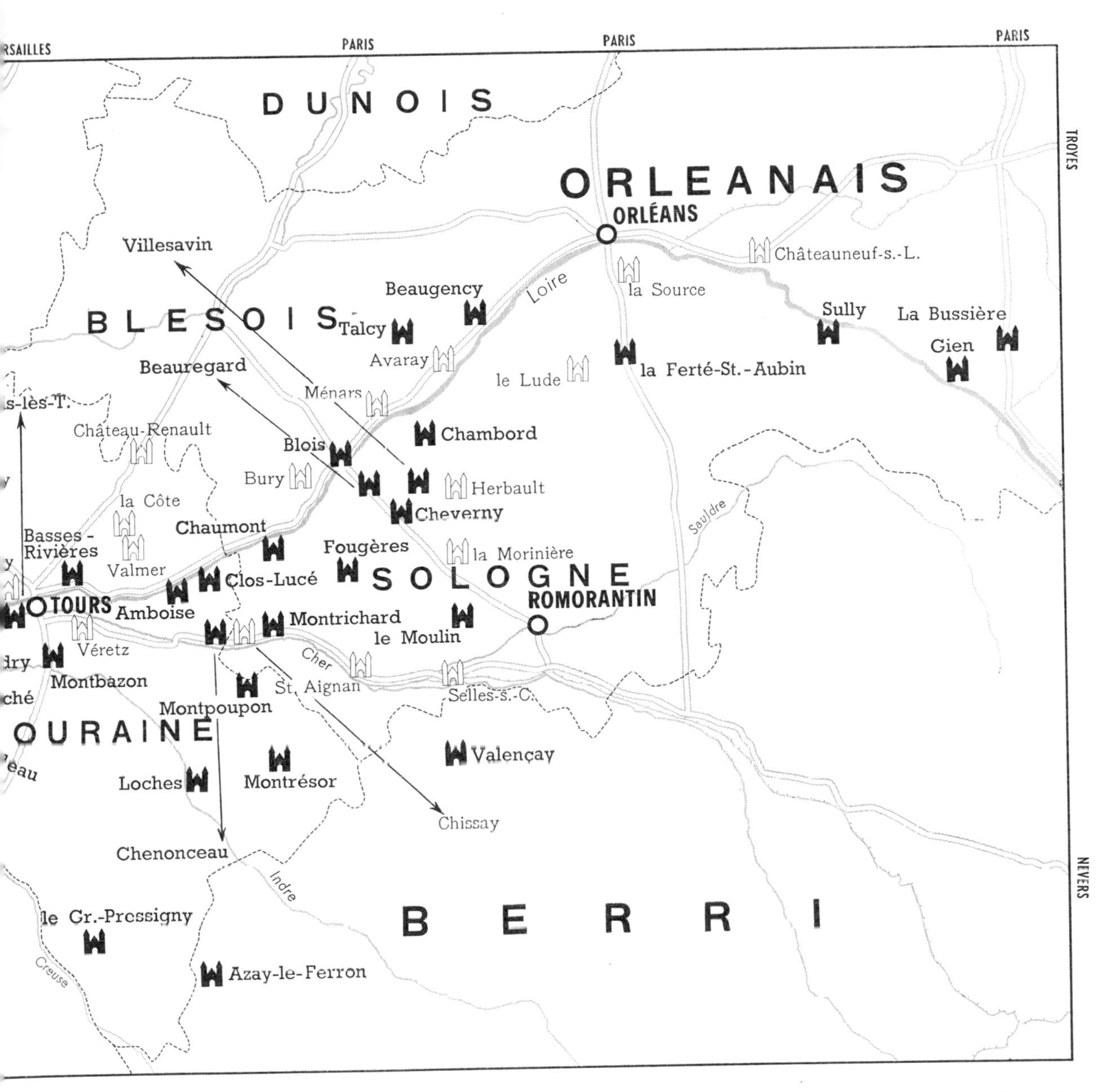

KEY: **Beaugency,** château mentioned in this work; Chissay, other châteaux; **ORLÉANS,** main town.

The 17th century was to see the partial rebuilding of Brissac, while the ancient estate of the Maillés, raised to a duchy, took the name of Luynes, victor over Concini. Shortly afterwards Cheverny was built, a symphony in white, a complete collection of décors; also the Gaston-d'Orléans wing at Blois, where François Mansard showed his severity and steadiness in the service of this scheming prince, often a coward yet with an endearing personality, who assembled splendid collections of works in the château to which the crown, tired of his intrigues, exiled him. Mansard also worked at La Ferté-Saint-Aubin, and his pupil, Le Muet, at Luynes.

This period also saw the tragi-burlesque episodes of the quarrel between the king, Louis XIII, and his mother: the imprisonment of the latter at Blois, her spectacular flight to Loches, reconciliation at the château of Couzière, near Tours, Marie de Médicis' installation at Angers, a new plot, the consequent mock battle at Ponts-de-Cé, a new reconciliation at Brissac, while waiting for the next intrigue... etc., etc., etc.

Richelieu, a great enemy of the fortified château, even though himself the proprietor of Chinon, spared the châteaux of the Val de Loire, but by destroying Cinq-Mars he made clear what punishment rebels might expect now that the authority of the monarch had become absolute. In the far south of Touraine he had an immense château built for himself, one he never visited and of which nothing remains to us today but a melancholy park.

At the end of March 1652, fleeing the Fronde, Louis XIV, Anne d'Autriche, Mazarin and the court sought refuge in the châteaux of Gien and Sully, where they were soon to receive a significant supporter, Turenne. Reconciled at Saumur with the child-monarch, the great general defeated Condé at Bléneau: once again victory smiled on the royal armies in the Val de Loire.

These successes caused Louis to quit the region, using its châteaux mainly as prisons. In the château of Nantes he imprisoned the Cardinal de Retz; Angers and Amboise he used to incarcerate Foucquet; Amboise again for Lauzun. However, he did return later to stay at Chambord, taking Molière with him. It was thus that characters like Monsieur de Pourceaugnac and Monsieur Jourdain (le bourgeois gentilhomme) were born on the banks of the Loire. But the king seemed to forget Blois, using it merely to get rid of a troublesome Queen of Poland.

Although it is more evident in the residences of Île-de-France and the mansions built in Paris, the 18th century did not disdain the Loire Valley. Stanislas Leczinski, the eternal wanderer, a king without a kingdom, installed himself at Chambord, although two years later the unhealthy stench from the moat forced him to leave during the summer for Blois and Ménars. He left the region to take possession of the crown of Lorraine, being replaced there, twelve years later, by the brother of his rival for the throne of Poland, the maréchal de Saxe, who lived an extraordinary life there, dying in 1750 in rather mysterious circumstances. It was a sign of the times when certain châteaux began to pass into the hands of rich financiers, such as Chenonceaux, acquired by Dupin, the farmer-general of revenues, who assembled an entire court of writers there, persuading Jean-Jacques Rousseau to come too.

New residences rose: Avaray, curiously constructed in the Louis XIII style; the little ' empty bottles ' of Basses-Rivières; Montgeoffroy, where the furnishings and appointments of the maréchal de Contades have been preserved intact; Chanteloup, where Choiseul collected a rebellious court and of which only the pagoda remains to us today; finally, Ménars, Mme de Pompadour's final ' workshop ', improved upon for her brother, the marquis de Marigny. At Villandry the Castellane family had some splendid landscape gardening done, which was pitilessly destroyed during the 20th century. Neo-classic art appeared on thc scene at Pignerolle, near Angers, where the directors of the riding academy had a copy of le Petit Trianon at Versailles built. Franklin resided at Chaumont.

Though it saved Blois, whose demolition had been ordered by Louis XVI, the French Revolution did not leave all the châteaux untouched, some measure of damage being done everywhere to any marks and emblems of royalty. In 1793, 2,000 rebels of La Vendée were shot in the château of Ponts-de-Cé. Many residences were converted into barracks or were deserted and left to fall into ruins, like Chinon. Sometimes their new owners had to face up to brutal decisions, such as the ex-consul Roger Ducos, who had three-quarters of the old château demolished.

Napoleon was interested in the Val de Loire only as somewhere where he could send the kings of Spain, who were imprisoned in the château of Valençay, in Talleyrand's charge, and he chose to wink at Mme de Stael's stay at Chaumont. Yet the château of Blois was to see the Empress and the roi de Rome early in April 1814, for it was there they spent the agonizing days of the collapse of the imperial régime. Marie-Louise's bearing during this time—as Monsieur André Castelot has shown—was far more dignified than it was later said to have been.

The 19th century saw the completion of Rochecotte, where Talleyrand received Balzac and passed his last summers, a survivor from the days of *la douceur de vivre*, while the Gothic troubadour appeared at the château des Hayes. We may also recall the last prisoners of these châteaux during this same century—the Duchesse de Berry, held at Nantes, and Abd el-Kader, held at Amboise—and recall that it witnessed numerous restorations which saved some of the châteaux from decline: Joly-Leterme at Montreuil-Bellay and Chinon, Jules Potier de La Morandière at Beauregard, Saint Aignan and Talcy, Lucien Roy at Langeais, Lucien Magne at Serrant, and Duban especially at Blois, all did work which was at times indiscreet, yet always conscientious and necessary. Anjou, on the other hand, Monsieur Pierre du Colombier has said, saw the building of a number of new châteaux in this period: La Jumellière, la Turmelière, Champtoceaux, proof of the nobility's ancestral attachment to the region, witnessed in another, more touching way, by the fact that Chambord was the name the last heir to the monarchy used until his death.

The early years of our own century saw the last builders or transformer of châteaux: Jacques Siegfried entirely refurnished and re-decorated Langeais; the de Broglie family removed the village around Chaumont, and created an immense park; Carvallo, a doctor, restored Villandry, surrounding it by admirable gardens. But since the inter-war period the state has had to undertake the maintenance of Azay-le-Rideau, Chaumont and Chambord.

Not all the collections of our national museums had arrived in their place of refuge on the banks of the Loire, in 1940, when the war caught up with them. It was at the château of Cangé, near Tours, that one of the most dramatic councils of ministers in our history was held, early in June. A few days later Amboise was hit by the bombardments and the château of Saumur witnessed the heroic efforts of the cadets of the cavalry school to defend the crossing of the Loire—too peaceful a river ever to have held back any army.

History—history in the grand sense—has now deserted these châteaux, which today are dedicated to art and tourism. Azay-le-Rideau and Chaumont, refurnished, Angers fitted out in a remarkable way to receive l'Apocalypse, Talcy restored and opened to the public, Gien transformed into a Museum of the Hunt, Plessis-lez-Tours remodelled, Basses-Rivières become a Wine Museum, and many others too, all these, illuminated against the night sky, prove the vitality of the Loire region in this domain and invite the visitor to come and make his own discoveries.

Gien.

The town of Gien suffered very heavily in 1940 and only the château survived almost intact from the bombardments. Today the château of Anne de Beaujeu, now transformed into a Museum of the Hunt. still raises its elegant silhouette of brick, with glazed decorative effects. against the sky, with the rebuilt church of St. Joan of Arc at its side and, below, the attractive little houses of the new Gien. Most of the right tower goes back as far as the 12th and 13th centuries. the rest of the buildings having been constructed for Anne de Beaujeu (1494-1500)

The Museum of the Hunt, housed in the château de Gien, has for some years now been the home of the series of paintings and sketches which François Desportes (1661-1743) did of the dogs belonging to the royal kennels, works which were formerly housed in the château of Compiègne. They will be found in the great hall, with its remarkable timber-work. Represented here are two lively still-lifes, both items in this collection.

Sully-sur-Loire.

The château of Sully, massive yet elegant, rises up on the banks of the river. Its various parts belong to different epochs: on the north side, facing the river, there is the 14th century château, flanked by four towers (see plate opposite), where Joan of Arc was received by Georges de La Trémoille. On the south side there is the entrance pavilion and the small 16th century château, remodelled by Sully, who had the Béthune tower, surrounded by moats, constructed (seen on the left of the photo above). The lower courtyard (seen here in the foreground) contains a statue of Sully and is itself entirely surrounded by moats. The interior, devastated in recent years by a search for a legendary treasure, is today in ruins.

Right: *Sully. The 14th Century Château.*

One will notice the lack of correspondence between the round way of the towers and that of the connecting ramparts. The windows were added later. The portions to the left of the second tower date from the 16th and 17th centuries.

La Ferté-Saint-Aubin.

The château de la Ferté, whose construction was spread over the centuries, shows a marked lack of homogeneity as a result. In the photo above, the most ancient part, dating from the 14th and 15th century, is seen on the left. It survived the reconstruction of the château, carried out between 1635 and 1650 to François Mansard's designs (section on the right). This section, built in brick and stone, with tall columns, was never completed. The park surrounding the château is all that remains of the former estate, which was sold and divided up in 1863.

Left: *La Bussière (Loiret).*

This château, built between the 13th and 17th centuries, is not very well known, its main attraction being its magnificent site, on the shore of a lake near the Forest of Orleans. The interior contains a prison and a courtroom.

Le Moulin.

Situated in the heart of Sologne, near the village of Lassay, the château of Moulin stands on a square 'terre-plein' surrounded by moats. The intention of the builders was no doubt to enclose the entire quadrangle by a curtain wall which was never completed. The imposing appearance of the entrance (see photo opposite) is not meant to create the impression of a truly fortified residence, these towers and the 'mâchicoulis' on the far tower serving at the time of construction (c. 1480-c. 1500) to indicate the noble rank of the proprietor, Philippe du Moulin. A contemporary mural in the neighbouring church at Lassay, featuring the château, shows that the entrance wing was remodelled and given larger windows some years later. The residence itself, with its dressing of red and black brickwork, communicates with a graceful little chapel in the flamboyant style.

Chambord.

On the preceding page is a view of the château seen from the park, the façade one sees on coming to the end of the avenue leading in from the entrance gates—an avenue three miles in length, cutting across the Forest of Chambord. This, however, is not the entrance façade of the château itself. Beyond a moat fed by the River Cosson and a garden, later redesigned, one sees the entire château, its north wall flanked by two towers, of which the one on the right houses the chapel. In the centre is the château proper, the keep, surrounded by four towers and composed of four sections topped by roofs in the French style. In the very centre of the keep rises the small lantern tower, over the staircase, a feature which dominates the entire structure.

On the front façade (see photo above), the ' enceinte ' has not been built higher than the ground floor. This is in order to leave the view across the forest free. The corner towers were, however, to have been the same as the towers at the rear yet were never completed. There is a striking resemblance between the plan of this château and that of the château of Vincennes.

Chambord, Interior.

Robbed of its furniture from the 18th century on, the château of Chambord is all but empty today. But in addition to the pieces of furniture, paintings and tapestries which have been exhibited there by the Department of Historical Monuments, there is this beautiful porcelain stove, installed by the maréchal de Saxe, who came to live at the château in 1748, living a life of luxury there until his death in 1750. Whether the hero died of congestion of the lungs or in a duel with the Prince de Conti is still a matter of argument.

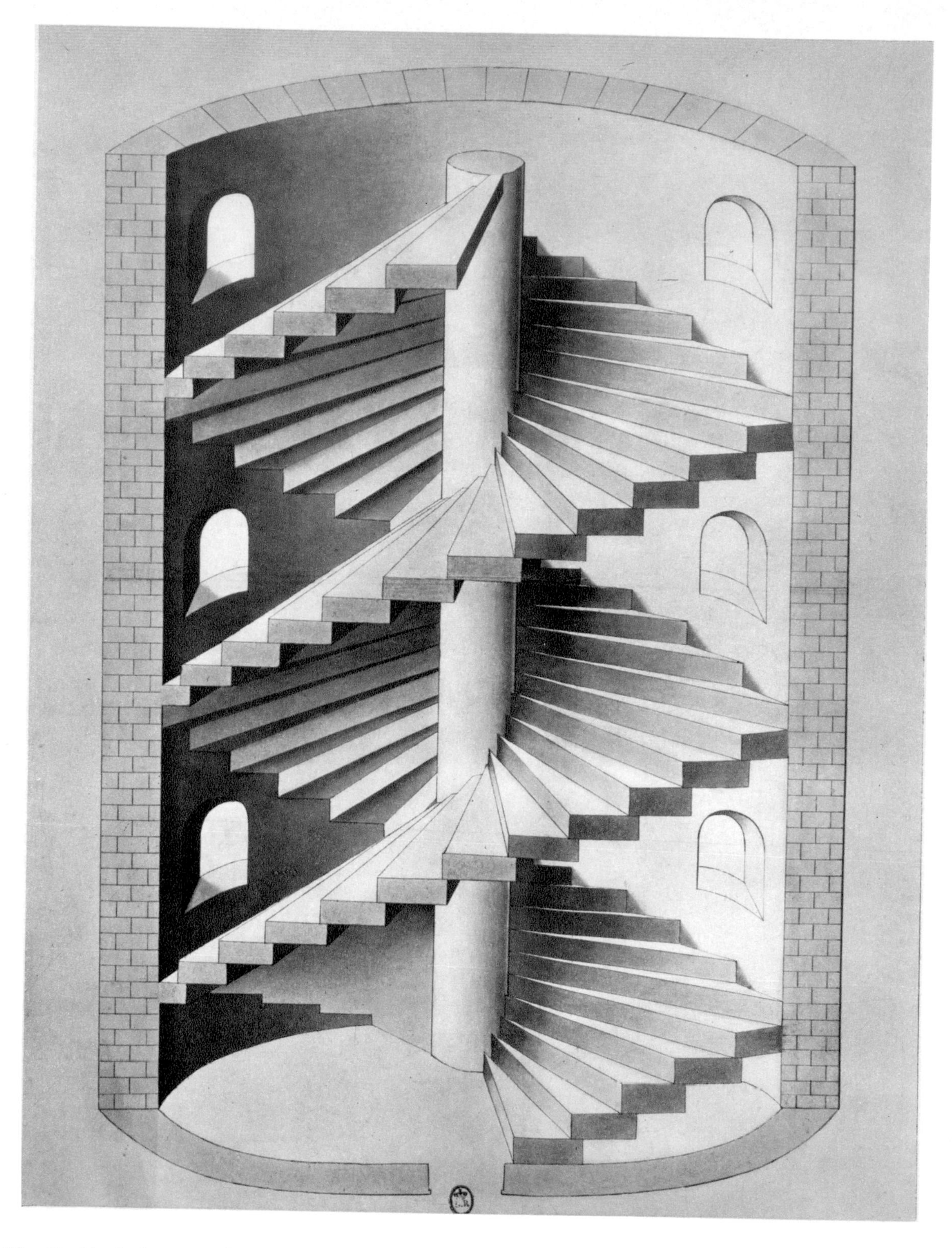

The Double Staircase at Chambord. (Drawing by an anonymous draughtsman, Bibliothèque Nationale).

The double spiral staircase at Chambord, situated in the very centre of the edifice and commanding its four sections, may have been conceived by Leonardo da Vinci, who died near Amboise in 1519. He may even have had a quadruple staircase in mind. Monsieur Gébelin supposes that after his death the masons substituted a double stair in a stairwell consisting of columns, the sides being left open.

The Lantern Tower.

Built of tufa stone inlaid with slate and with a fleur de lys on the summit, the lantern tower of the spiral staircase, surrounded by buttressing arches, dominates a veritable forest of elaborate chimneys rising up from the roofs of Chambord.

Right: *Detail of Sculpture.*

Leaving the façades of the château, with their rhythmic lines of pillars, in all the grandeur of their simplicity, the artists of Chambord placed their sculpture in positions where it could be seen from close to. For example, along the staircases, where an imagination largely coloured by Italian ideas was given full rein. (Some of the sculpture was often restored during the 19th century).

Chambord.

Here the crowned salamander, emblem of François I, is seen enclosed within an elegant ring of flames.

Talcy.

There is no doubt that this château was built at the end of the 15th century. The entrance tower (keep) may have kept its ' mâchicoulis ' and the double gate, in the medieval manner, yet this is mainly for the sake of décor and appearance. The absence of a moat proves this; to be allowed to construct one was a noble privilege and it may be that this privilege was not granted to the first proprietor.

Talcy.

The interior of Talcy, acquired by the State as late as 1933, has preserved the charm of an inhabited home. Successive generations brought this furniture here and the aim of the present (State) administration has been to leave everything exactly as it was. *Above:* the bedroom known as that of Catherine de Médicis, with canopy and headboard in painted silk and, at the side, a Flemish tapestry. The armchairs date from the French Regency (Louis XIV) period and have been recovered in Aubusson tapestry.

Right: The main drawing-room, decorated with an Aubusson tapestry dating from the 17th century and depicting *The Birth of Bacchus.* The carpet is from the 'La Savonnerie' workshop and of the Louis XVI period.

Beaugency.

This engraving by Claude de Chastillon, dating from the early years of the 17th century, shows the keep of Beaugency, dominating the fortified bridge. Built at the end of the 11th century and reinforced with flat buttresses, the keep, which has scarcely changed in outward appearance, has five floors, the vaults of which collapsed during the 19th century. On the right, the engraver has featured an imaginative version of Dunois' château, built in the 15th century and today the home of a museum. On the left: the fortified bridge, at the time the only bridge across the Loire between Blois and Orléans.

Beauregard.

This engraving by Du Cerceau shows us Beauregard as it was before the reconstructions carried out during the 19th century. Built between 1522 and 1554 by Jean du Thier, secretary of state to Henri II, and possibly to plans by Philibert Delorme, it consists mainly of a gallery joining two pavilions. The decoration, of pillars and medallions, is very simple. In this engraving one will notice the old gardens, in the 16th century style, and, on the right, the 'colombier'—pigeon house—a seigniorial privilege. In our day the building at the back has been concealed behind a new wing, while that on the right has disappeared. The left wing has remained more or less intact but now has larger windows.

Beauregard, Interiors.

Above: panel in the first floor gallery, a detail from the lower half of the wainscoting, possibly older than the rest of the château. It depicts the porcupine, emblem of Louis XII, with the motto: *Cominus et eminus* (From near and far), refering to the belief that the porcupine could shoot its darts at its enemies from a distance.

Left: the *des Grelots* room, a remnant of the 1554 decoration ordered by Scibec: timberwork in the form of decorated panels, below: reliefs and coats of arms (of the Du Thier family, proprietors of the château), and above: painted panels representing still-lifes relevant to the master's activities: here we see tennis racquets and balls.

Beauregard: The Garden Front.

The two outer pavilions are still more or less as they were in the 16th century, despite the added profusion of dormer-windows; but the central wing, a modern construction, has been added to the original gallery, thus completely changing the proportions of the château and the silhouette presented by its roofs.

Beauregard.

The first-floor gallery, decorated in the early 17th century to the orders of Ardier, a judge, is lined entirely with Delftware tiles, each of which represents a soldier or non-commissioned officer in the various regiments of Louis XIII's time: cavalry, artillery, infantry, musketeers, pike-men, standard-bearers, all arranged in regulation order.

Blois in the 18th Century (engraving by Jacques Rigaud).

On the right one sees the François I wing, with its open staircase, from which the statues had already disappeared. They were restored under the supervision of Duban in the 19th century (*see page 44*). At the rear of the courtyard: the Gaston-d'Orléans wing, a work of François Mansard. On the ground floor one notices the semi-circular colonnade, a style elegantly employed by the architect at Berny. On the left: the so-called Charles-d'Orléans wing, with its built-in arcade, which Rigaud has represented as intact, whereas it is supposed to have been removed by Duban. At the rear, the Saint-Calais chapel, the nave of which had been demolished by François Mansard. One will notice the simplicity of the architecture of this wing, devoid of all sculpture, even on the capitals of its columns.

Left: Detail of the outer façade of the Louis XII wing. The statue of the king, done by Seurre in 1857, has replaced the original statue, which will doubtlessly have been by Guido Mazzoni, an Italian artist Charles VIII brought back with him to France. This latter statue, of which the present one is a faithful copy, was destroyed during the Revolution, in 1792. Below it one sees the porcupine and crown, emblem of Louis XII, with the monograms of the king and of Anne de Bretagne on either side. The rest of the façade seems to have been wholly inspired by the flamboyant style, a reaction to the Italian influence. All this decoration was drastically restored by Duban during the 19th century.

Above: *Blois, the Gallery Façade.*

Backing on to the old ramparts, this elegant façade, very clearly influenced by the work Bramante did for the Vatican, represents one of the newest ideas in French Renaissance architecture. As Monsieur Gébelin has pointed out, however, instead of erecting tiers of ornamental arcading, the French masons have built a thick wall punctuated by deep ' boxes '. On the second floor, the second and third windows from the right are those of the king's room in which the duc de Guise was assassinated. The attic floor, built no doubt under Catherine de Médicis, was added later, which explains the irregularity of the gargoyles and the slope of the roof.

Left: *Blois, the Saint-Calais Chapel.*

All that remains since the 17th century of this graceful little chapel, built during the reign of Louis XII and consecrated in 1508, is the choir, recently restored and provided with modern windows. The old choir screen has been preserved in the museum.

Above: *Blois, a Section of the Courtyard.*

From right to left: The Louis XII wing, with the staircase pavillon, the State Room (13th century), where the Estates General met in 1576 and 1588, and the François I wing. A comparison with the engraving on page 41 reveals that the ground floor on the left was remodelled by Duban.

Right: *Blois, Interior.*

The château's interior decoration was largely demolished during the 18th and 19th centuries, when the building was transformed into a barracks. Even the chimneys were destroyed to make more room. It was restored during the 19th century by Duban, very conscientiously yet with a rather heavy hand. However, this stone chimneypiece, decorated with François I's salamander and the ermine of Claude de France, is the original one, which Duban had re-painted and re-gilded.

Above: *Blois, Detail of the François I Staircase.*

The outside ramps of the staircase also served as balconies, where leading members of the court stood to watch tourneys held in the courtyard. It was here, too, that the Swiss Guards stood whenever the king used the staircase. On the upper balustrade in this photo can be seen the initial letter F, with a crown and the salamander, the emblems of François I. The statue in the niche is the work of Seurre (1847).

Right: *Blois, Small Room Said To Be That of Catherine de Médicis.*

The left portion of the decoration dates from Catherine de Médicis' time, the *motifs*, seeming to have been cut out and applied to the background irrespective of the fall of light, being typical of the period. The chimneypiece and ceiling are the work of Duban.

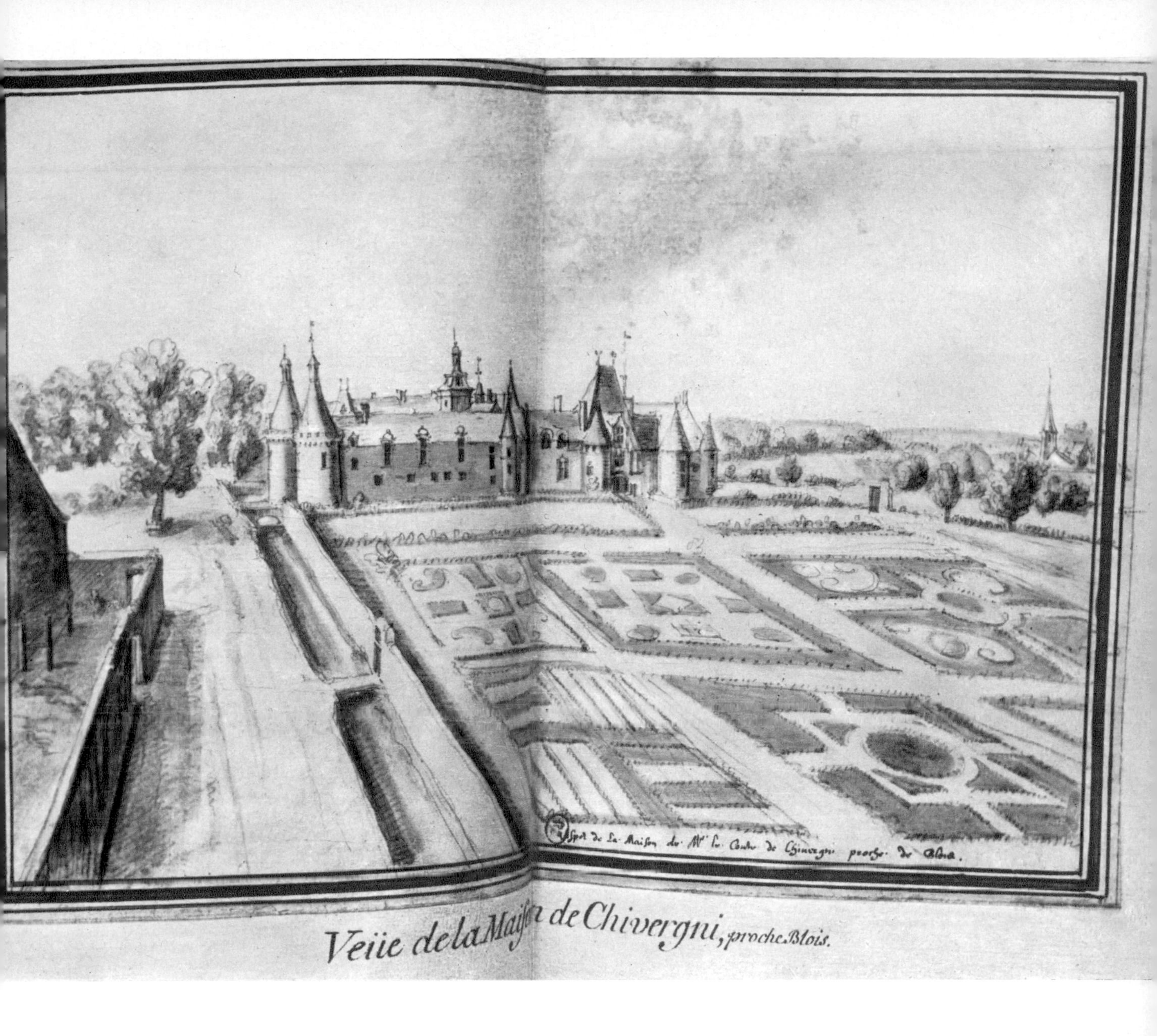

The First Château de Cheverny (Bibliothèque Nationale).

Where the present château stands there was, in the 16th century, another, with corner towers, of which we can obtain some idea from a drawing by Martellange (above) dating from the early 17th century. This would be the house Raoul Hurault built at the beginning of the 16th century, yet this drawing does not tally as regards the present outhouses, which are thought to be remnants of the first château de Cheverny.

Left: Detail from a Flemish tapestry, based on a Teniers cartoon, which hangs in the small drawing-room of the present château.

Cheverny.

The new château, built between 1629 and 1634 under Jacques Bougier's supervision, marks the transition from one age to another. Whereas the division into five main blocks, the sober façade with its pattern of parallel horizontal lines, and the square-based domes symbolize the 17th century, the narrowness of the central pavilion and the fact that it houses the staircase hark back to the Renaissance design. (This same arrangement will be found in the château of Mesnilvoisin in Île de France, built in the same period). Between the windows on the first floor are twelve oval niches, containing busts of the Roman emperors.

Right: The grand staircase, consisting of straight flights separated by arcades, entirely of stone, is typical of the period and goes back to the Henri II staircase in the Louvre. Notice beneath the second flight seen on this photograph the sculpture work, of flowers, fruits, and scrolls, embodying the initial letters C (for Cheverny), H (Hurault) and C (Chabot).

Cheverny, Interior Decoration.

The interior at Cheverny comprises a very extensive collection of early 17th decorative art. The ceilings of sculpted panels and the painted doors and wainscots, decorated with arabesques, show off the paintings in moulded frames above the doors and also the tapestries which adorn the walls.

Above: The King's Bedroom, decorated with a set of tapestries from the banks of the Bièvre, based on designs by Simon Vouet and representing the story of Ulysses. The bed-hangings and covers are of 16th century Persian cloth. The ceiling, illustrating the story of Perseus and the Medusa, and the wainscot, illustrating the story of Theagenes and Chariclea, were painted by le Blésois Monier.

Right: The great drawing-room, with a chimneypiece with sculpted figures of Fame, flanking a portrait attributed to Mignard of the Countess of Cheverny. The entire décor of this room is a 19th century reconstitution, embodying some genuine panels from earlier periods. The excellent Louis XIV chairs are covered with Aubusson tapestry.

Above: *Villesavin, Pedestal of Fountain.*

The fountain at Villesavin, which bears a relation to two basins coming from Gaillon (Louvre and château de la Rochefoucauld) may be a product of the Val de Loire or not. It is uncertain. While the basin itself and its lower portion might suggest a Florentine influence, this triangular socle—clearly Italianate in spirit and possibly from Genoa—has been fashioned in broad, flowing lines which are wholly French.

Left: *Villesavin, Chapel Wing.*

Built about the year 1537 for Jean le Breton, who supervised the building operations at Chambord, this charming little manor-house in the shape of a horse-shoe consists of a ground floor supporting a tall, steep roof. The pavilion at the end contains a chapel, decorated with frescoes. In the centre, a fine Renaissance fountain.

Valençay.

Beautifully sited on a low hill overlooking the valley of the Nahon and surrounded by a park inhabited by fallow deer, cranes and flamingoes, the château of Valençay consists of a series of buildings disposed at right-angles to each other. On the photo above we see: (from left to right): the small tower and low wing (about 1570), the main tower (keep), which dates from about 1560, the west wing and the big tower (about 1540), the south wing (17th century) and the Neuve tower (18th century).

Left: *Valençay.*

The most celebrated proprietor of the château was the Prince de Talleyrand, who acquired it in 1803. His portrait in court attire (a replica of a work by Gérard) is seen opposite. It is on display in the museum housed in the outbuildings.

Valençay, Southern Corner.

The south wing, dating from the 17th century, saw its courtyard drastically restyled in the 18th century by de Villemorien who built the tower on the left, the Neuve tower.

Fougères-sur-Bièvre, Interior Courtyard.

Even though the towers of this small château have still retained a medieval touch, one notices how due to the influence of the Charles-d'Orléans gallery at Blois a gallery has been introduced here, too, similar to those that will be found at Beaugency and Talcy.

Above: *Montpoupon.*

Remote from the main highways, the château of Montpoupon has 15th and 16th century residential quarters attached to a fine keep belonging to the 13th century. It looks down upon three valleys fed by five streams.

Left: *Fougères-sur-Bièvre, Interior Courtyard.*

The living quarters are on the left, their various floors being reached by a staircase contained with a tower with minute 16th century windows flanked by small pillars on either side.

Chaumont.

Notwithstanding the drawbridge's chains, the towers about the entrance to the château have nothing military about them. Their walls are decorated with the armorial bearings of Pierre d'Amboise and with mountains covered with flames (*chaud mont*), the emblems of the house.

Right: The foundations of the north wing, demolished during the 18th century, afford a wide view over the Loire. The Italian well is a 20th century addition.

Chaumont.

Page 64: The chapel was built in the 15th and 16th centuries, the vaulted ceiling being 17th century work. The middle window is flanked by two 15th century carved triptychs, either of Flemish or German origin.

Page 65: The front façade, containing the entrance gate.

Above: The interior of the château has been decorated with Renaissance furniture from the reserve collection of the musée de Cluny. This bedroom is called the 'Catherine de Médicis room'.

Amboise, Seen from the Island in the Loire.

Behind the houses on the river bank, rebuilt after the war, we see the grand terrace, flanked by towers, from which rise the buildings comprising the château. In the middle: the Minimes tower, containing a spiral ramp permitting access by carriage to the château terrace, and the royal apartments with the balcony on which the conspirators of 1560 were hanged. On the right: the Saint-Hubert Chapel.

Amboise, State Room.

This room occupies the entire second floor of the royal apartments, built during the reign of Charles VIII. Transformed into apartments for the Emir Abd el-Kader during the 19th century, it was restored by Rupricht-Robert in 1908. With thick walls of brick and stone, its ceiling consists of two lines of Gothic vaults supported down the middle of the hall by elegant little columns with richly embellished capitals, decorated alternatively with *fleurs de lys* and an ermine *motif*. On the mantelpiece (*left*) the same decorative *motif* occurs, accompanied by the arms of France and Brittany supported by two cherubs. The windows on the right look out on the balcony where the Amboise conspirators were hanged.

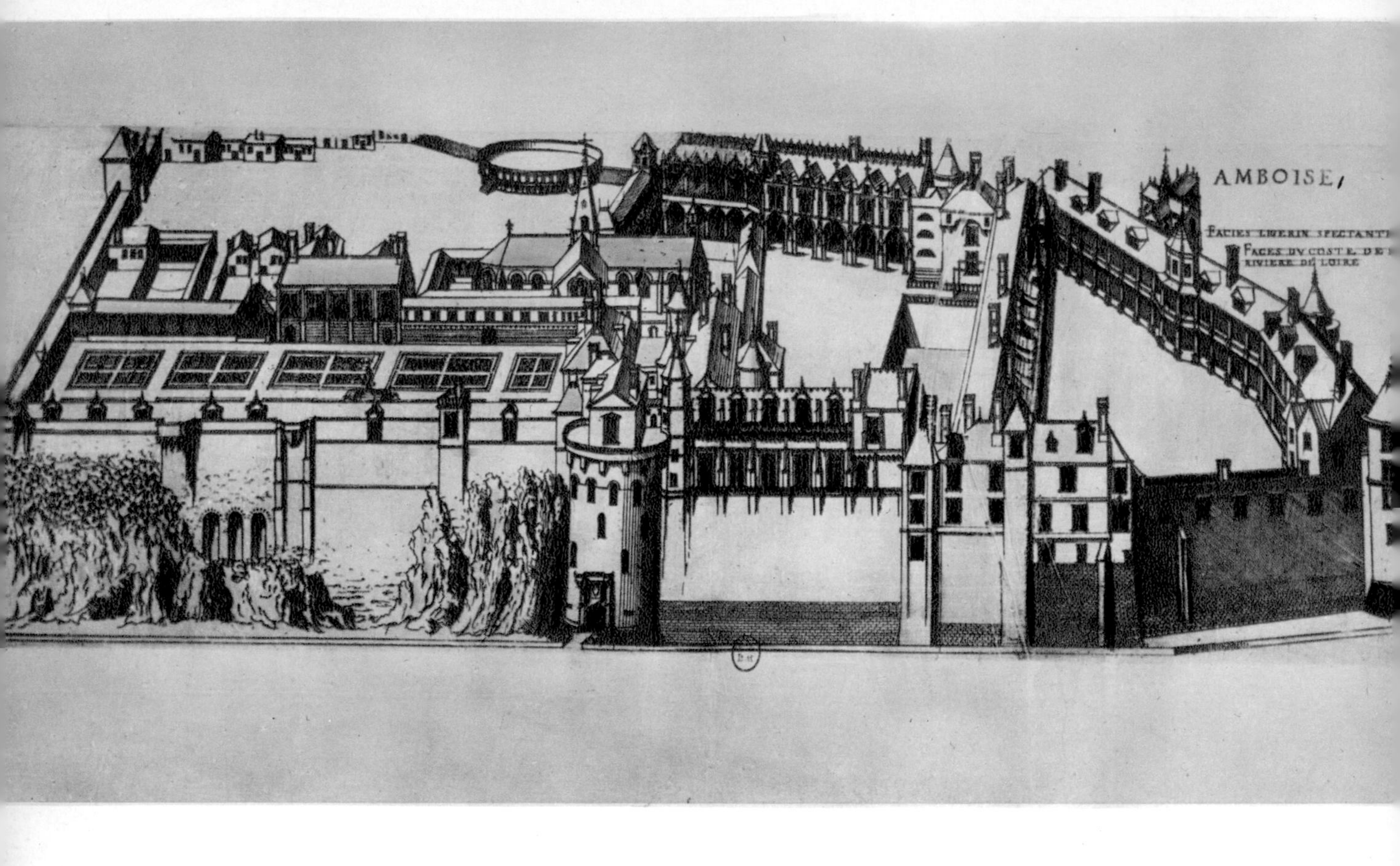

Amboise, General Views.

Du Cerceau's 16th century engraving makes clear how extensive the original château was, also the extent of the demolitions carried out to the ex-consul Roger Ducos' orders during the 19th century. A comparison with the aerial photograph on pages 70-71 shows that of the buildings in the foreground on the engraving above, all that remain are the front of the ramparts, the Minimes tower, the royal apartments and, behind them, the Louis XII wing (the building with a sloping roof on each side and flanked by a bell-turret). Of the buildings in the background: the Saint-Hubert chapel, next to the word 'Amboise', the Heurtault tower and, on the left, the rampart. On this engraving we can also see the gardens designed by the Neapolitan gardener, Pacello da Mercogliano.

Right: The Charles VIII wing on the left and the Louis XII wing on the right. Notice the way in which the dormer windows have developed.

Amboise, the Saint-Hubert Chapel.

Built at the end of the 15th century, to the orders of Charles VIII, the chapel shows a marked Flemish influence, especially in the sculpted stone frieze running all round the building, with small figures among the delicate ornamental arcading (see photo on right). It is reminiscent of Brabantine retables. A great deal of restoration work was done in the chapel during the 19th century.

Clos-Lucé (Amboise).

It was in this house, built during Louis XI's reign, that Leonardo da Vinci died in 1519. The house contains a small museum devoted to the artist. Recently 16th century frescoes were discovered here and the mouth of a tunnel leading to the château of Amboise.

Montrésor.

Ranged around a rocky promontory, a wall of the old fortress still remains, flanked by partially demolished towers. Its oldest parts date back to the last years of the 10th century.

Above: *Azay-le-Ferron.*

From left to right, one sees: the arcaded gallery (modern), the round tower built in 1496, the Humières wing built in 1638, and the François I pavilion, built at the beginning of the 16th century.

Pages 78-79: *Chissay.*

Built by Charles VII on an attractive site overlooking the valley of the Cher, the château of Chissay was completed in the 16th and 17th centuries.

Azay-le-Ferron, Grand Dining-Room.

The tapestry (Aubusson) is based on Oudry's *Louis XV Hunting Scenes* and is flanked by two chandeliers. Louis XV cartel clock; on the table, silver candelabra (English silverware of the early 19th century).

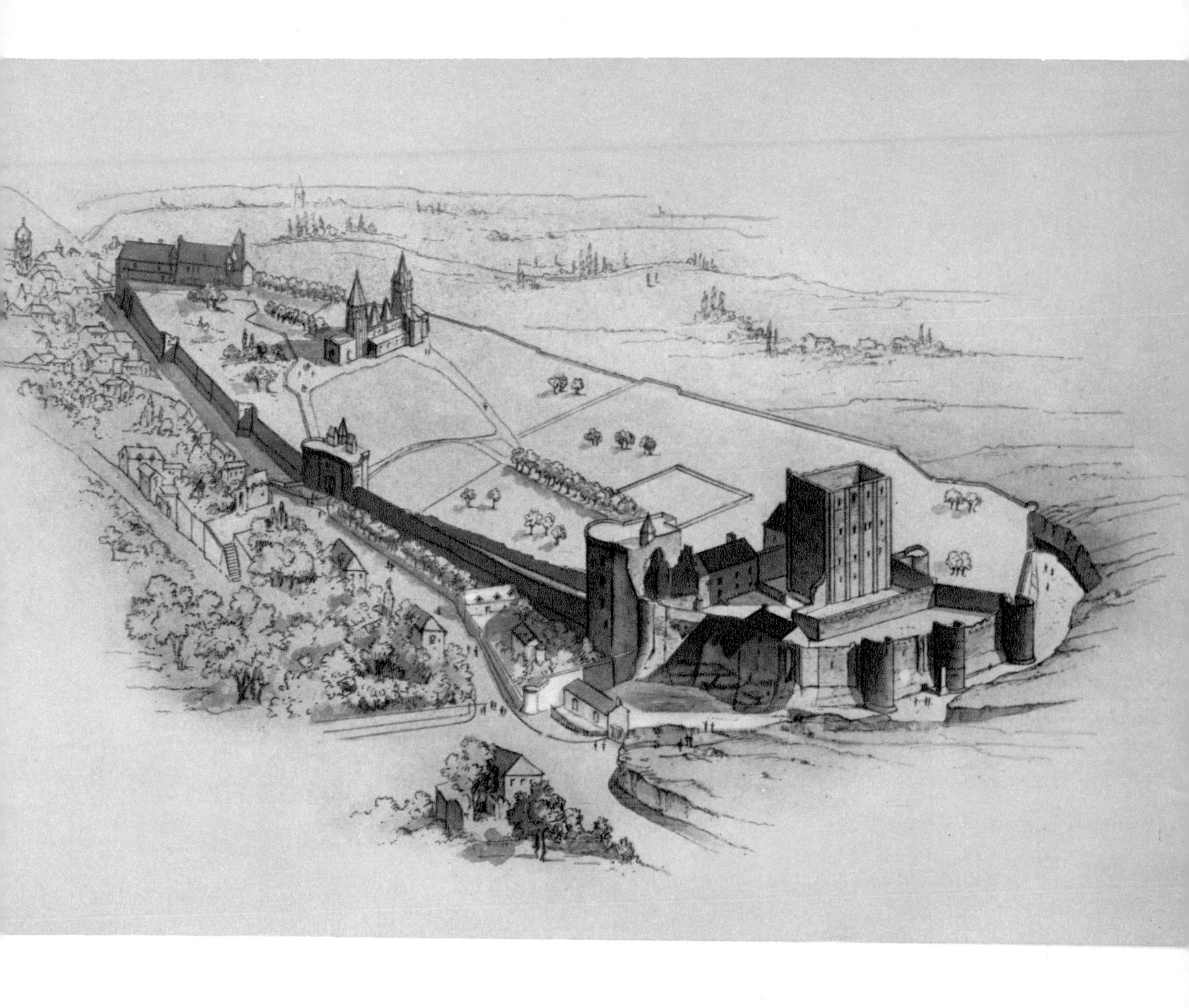

Above: *Loches, General Prospect (based on a relief in the keeping of the Department of Historical Monuments).*

The château of Lochés occupies the entire top of a hill situated between the valley of the Indre and a nearby valley. From left to right on this drawing: the royal apartments, the château gate, the church of Saint-Ours, the Round Tower, the forge and the keep.

Left: *Le Grand-Pressigny.*

Le Grand-Pressigny, an ancient fortress of which the dungeon tower still survives, was rebuilt from the middle of the 16th century on by Honorat de Savoie, marquis de Villar. The country-house which resulted abuts onto the Vironne tower, a curious watch-tower crowned by ' mâchicoulis ' and a dome.

Loches, South Front.

The fortress's weakest point was south of the 'enceinte', on the side of the plain. Its main defences have therefore been massed on this spot. Here the square keep, an 11th century structure, can be seen. It was surrounded later on by a rampart with almond-shaped towers. This part of the château was not used, except as a prison from Louis XI's reign onwards.

Right: *Loches, Private Chapel of Anne de Bretagne.*

In the northern section of the royal apartments, the part known as the *vieilles salles*, which was built during Louis XII's reign, will be found this charming little private chapel decorated with ermine *motifs* and cord and tassel designs, the emblems of Anne of Brittany.

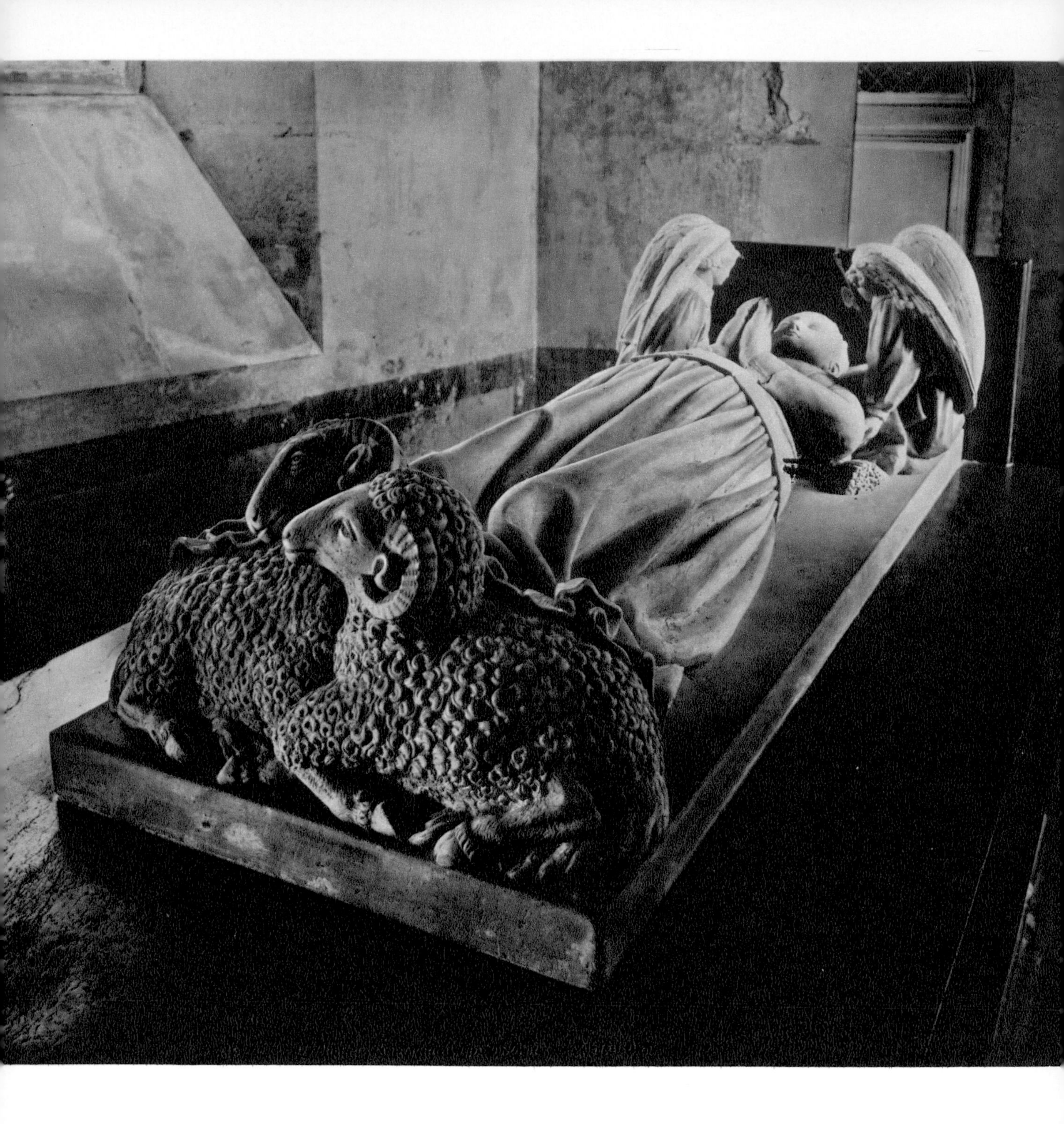

Loches, Tomb of Agnès Sorel.

Agnès Sorel, who may have lived at Loches with Charles VII, died at Mesnil-sous-Jumièges and was buried in the middle of the choir of the collegiate church of Saint-Ours. During the reign of Louis XVI the canons were authorized to remove the tomb, which was taken to the château in 1809, being placed on the ground floor of the Agnès Tower. The recumbent statue, which is attributed to the Provençal sculptor, Jacques Morel (c. 1395-1459), is of the king's favourite, her feet resting on two sheep symbolizing her Christian name.

Chenonceaux, Seen from the Avenue of Approach.

Beyond the pair of Louis XVI sphinxes (which come, it is said, from Chanteloup) we see the keep or Marques Tower, a 15th century edifice, in the foreground right—the only remnant of the original château. Beyond it rises the new château, built by Thomas Bohier on the banks of the River Cher subsequent to 1515.

Chenonceaux.

The ' terre-plein ' of the château is surrounded by moats fed by the waters of the Cher, which flow past the Marques Tower (*see photo opposite*) and frame the formal gardens which Diane de Poitiers had laid out. The owners of the loveliest gardens in Touraine sent the favourite samples of their rare flowers and vegetables, such as melons and artichokes. Catherine de Médicis continued this work. It was she who had the symmetrical garden seen above laid out. It was Diane de Poitiers, too, who had the bridge built across the River Cher about 1555 (*see pages 90-91*), its architect, Philibert Delorme, intending this to be covered by a gallery of lower elevation than the present one. This gallery was built later, about 1580, for Catherine de Médicis, the architect in this case being Denis Cerutin. It is sober in style, leaning towards classicism, and very different indeed from Thomas Bohier's château. On the extreme left the unfinished stonework shows that Catherine was planning to have another building erected on the other bank of the river, symmetrical with the old château. The latter (*on the right*) stands on the piles of an old mill in the basement of which the kitchen and other servant's rooms are located. The library and chapel rise up from the breakwaters of the arch on which the château stands.

Chenonceaux, Interior: the Chapel in the 19th Century (romanticizing lithograph in the Bibliothèque Nationale).

Situated on a breakwater of the bridge over the Cher (*see pages 90-91*), the chapel shows clear signs in its decoration and ceiling of the late flamboyant period. There are some interesting graffiti on the walls.

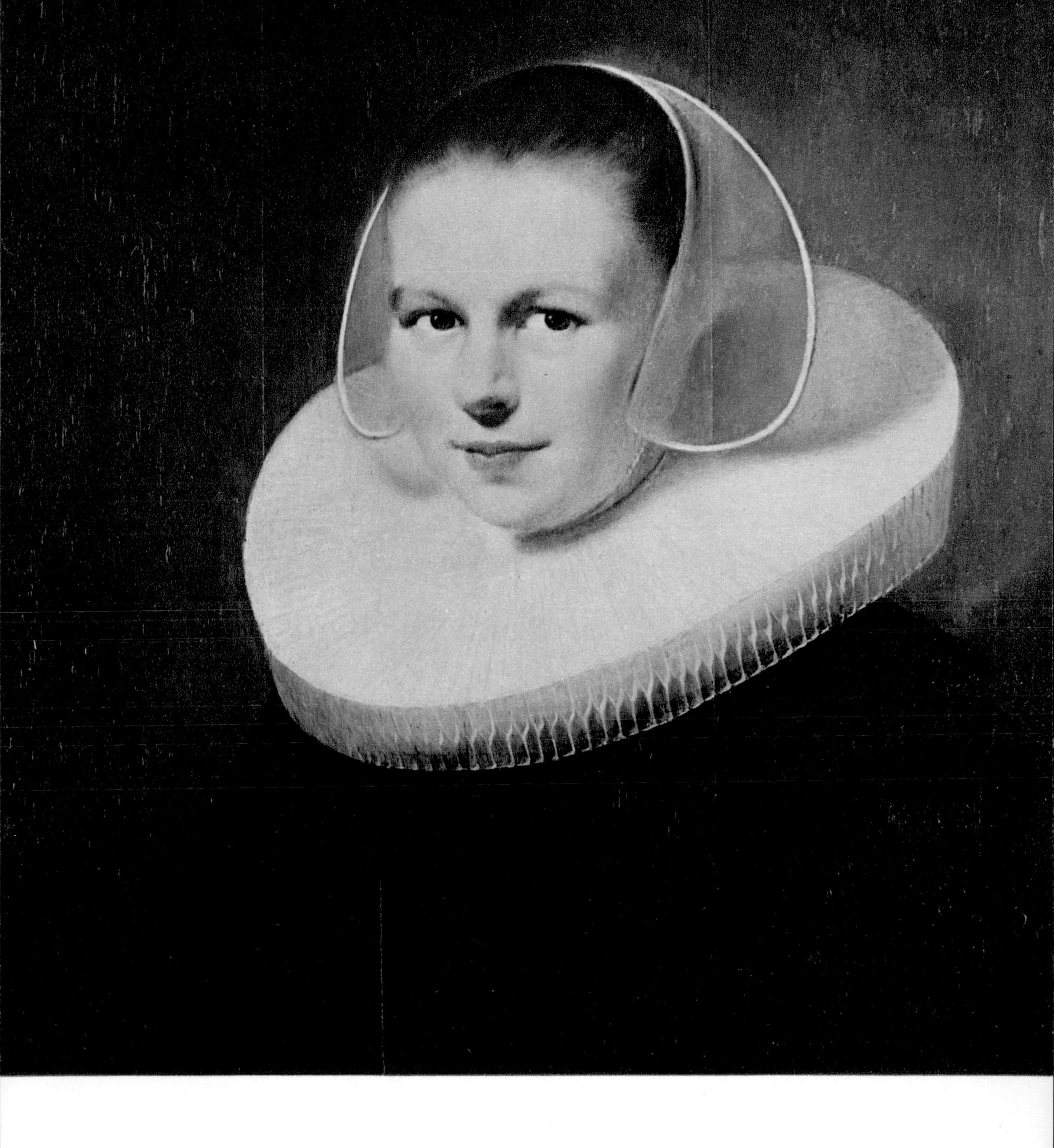

Chenonceaux, Interior: Portrait of a Woman, by Mirevelt (1567-1641).

This painting, in the François I bedroom, is one of several attractive works of art the château possesses, most of them collected by Mme Pelouze, a 19th century proprietor of the château.

Cinq-Mars.

Only two towers, an 11th century one (on right) and a 12th century one (on left), remain of the château in which Henry de Ruzé, marquis of Cinq-Mars, was born, their windows having been added during the 15th century. After the marquis' execution the château was demolished at Richelieu's orders.

Basses-Rivières (Rochecorbon).

This small country house, known in French as a 'vide-bouteilles', was built during the 18th century for the Papillon family, rich inhabitants of Touraine. Bequeathed to the city of Tours, it now houses an interesting museum on the subject of the vine and the wines of Touraine. This is Vouvray wine country.

Plessis-lez-Tours in the 17th Century (Aquarelle in the Gaignières Collection, Bibliothèque Nationale).

This 1699 view of the château shows us what it looked like as rebuilt by Louis XI about the year 1470. The royal apartments, are shown here in the foreground, situated on the left of the entrance. Nowadays all that remains of this complex is the southern part of the main building, that is to say, the right portion of the wing at the rear of the water-colour reproduced above (*see also page 96*). The aquarelles in the Gaignières Collection appertaining to the Val de Loire were done by Boudan in 1699, in the presence of the collector, François Roger de Gaignières (1642-1715).

Plessis-lez-Tours, Interior.

The château was transformed in the 19th century. Today, on the ground floor, the large painting of the *Last Judgement* (*see page 97*) is on view. It belongs in the chapel, in the left wing (on page 98). This canvas, directly related to François Loris' triptych of Notre-Dame-des-Sablons in the Brussels Museum, appears to have been executed by Jérôme Francken, a pupil of Loris, who spent some time in Touraine.

Above: Detail of sculpture, post-Louis XI, representing the ermine of Bretagne, emblem of Anne de Bretagne and Claude de France.

Villandry.

Built between 1532 and 1536, and already displaying certain characteristics of the second Renaissance as regards arrangement and style, Villandry was transformed on a considerable scale in the 18th century. It was restored to its original state by Dr. Carvallo, who had splendid gardens in the Renaissance style (*pages 100 and 102*) redesigned all round the château. On the photo opposite, one can see the 12th century keep, in which Philippe Auguste and Henry II of England signed their peace treaty in 1189, and also, on the extreme right of the photo, a small 18th century pavilion.

Villandry.

The façades of the ' cour d'honneur ' seem more ornate than the exterior, but this is sometimes due to recent restoration work. On the other hand, the corner towers have disappeared for good, being replaced by square pavilions, influenced by the Île-de-France style, says Monsieur Gébelin, in particular, that of Ecouen.

Montbazon. (Lithograph by Langlumé, Bibliothèque Nationale).

The great conqueror and builder, Foulque Nerra, comte d'Anjou, having captured Montbazon in the Blésois region, soon got on with the work of building a square keep there towards the end of the 10th century. This was then surrounded by a square 'enceinte', the remnants of which, clearly apparent in this 19th century, are still to be seen today. The tower, used in the previous century for Claude Chappe's telegraph, is surmounted nowadays by a large Second Empire statue of the Virgin Mary in regrettable taste.

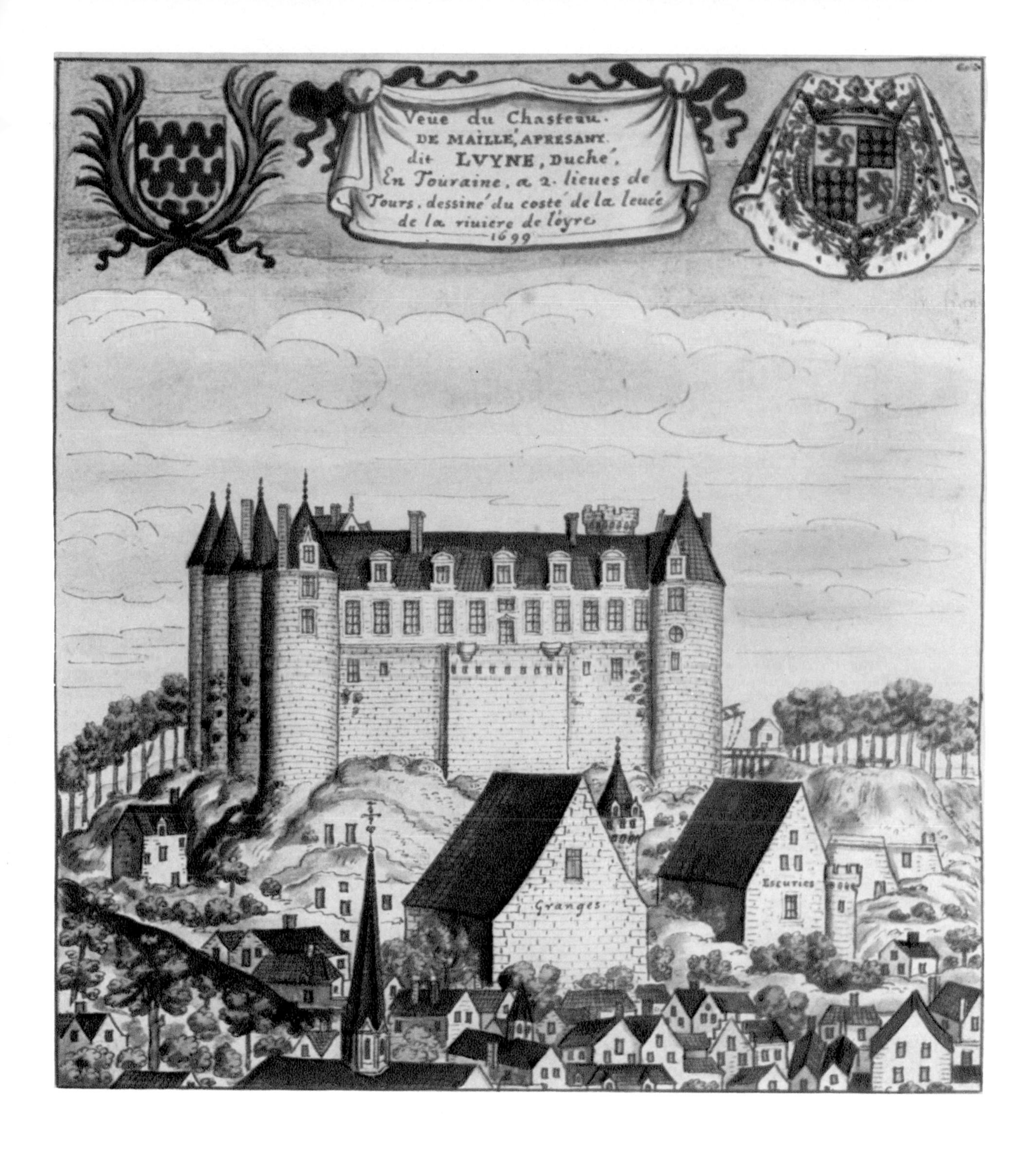

Luynes in the 17th Century (Aquarelle in the Gaignières Collection, Bibliothèque Nationale).

The fortress of Maillé, built in the 12th and 13th centuries for the family of the same name, was raised to a duchy for Charles d'Albert de Luynes during the reign of Louis XIII and took his name. It was he who had the wing seen above (built about 1650 by Le Muet) added on the south front. It was demolished during the 19th century—to open up the view on to the Loire, as at Chaumont and Ussé—and only the outer pavilions now remain. The coat of arms on the left of the title above is that of the Maillé family.

Pages 106-107: the west front, to which the windows were added during the 15th century.

Saché.

This 16th century château, remodelled during the 17th and 18th centuries, is famous above all, because Balzac used often to visit his friend, Monsieur de Margonne, there. Donated to the Department of Indre-et-Loire by Monsieur Paul Métadier, today it houses a museum. The windows have lost their mullions and the stairway hall its lantern roof.

Azay-le-Rideau. →

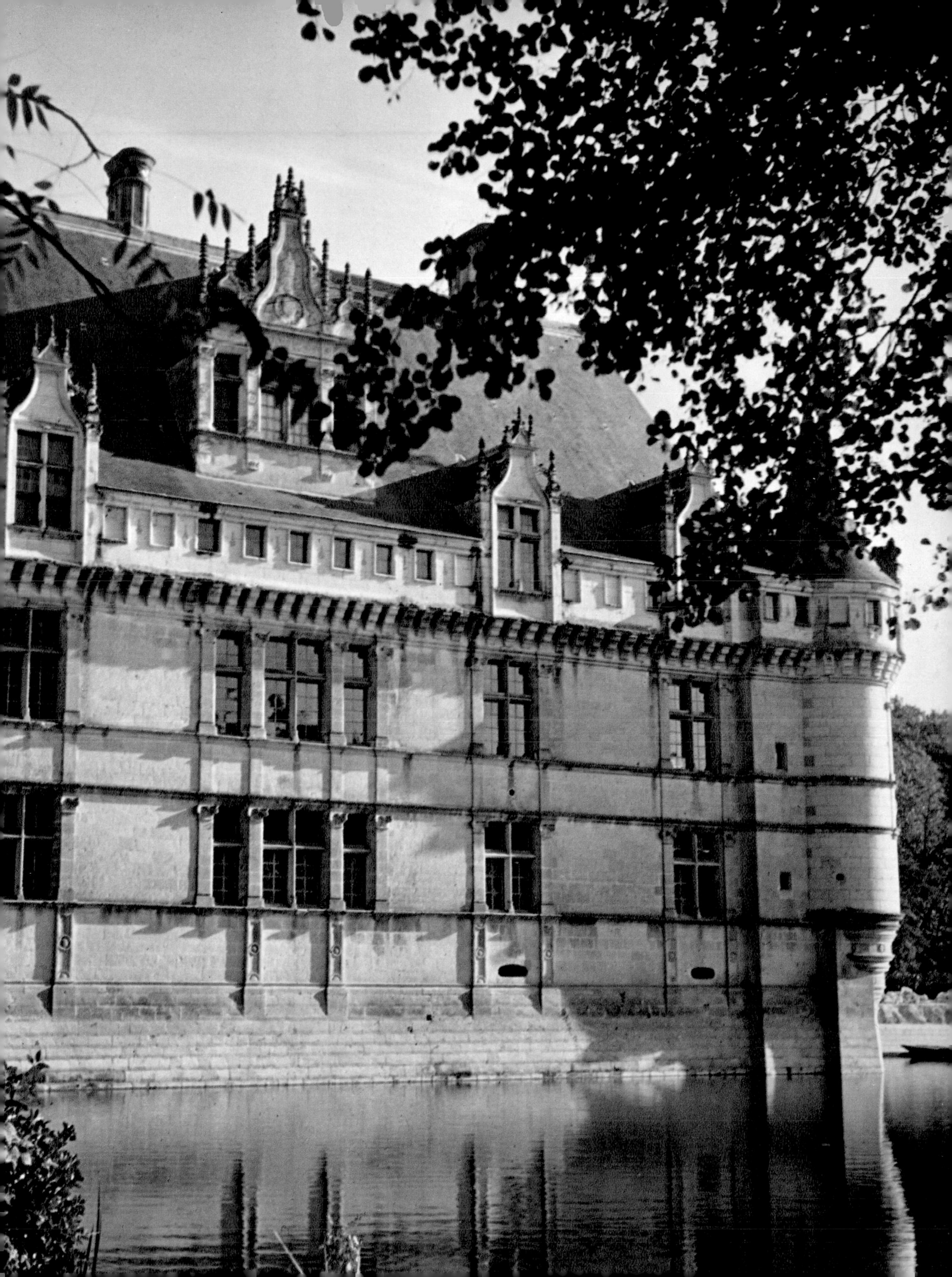

Azay-le-Rideau in the 19th Century (Lithograph by Langlumé, Bibliothèque Nationale).

Gilles Berthelot, treasurer of France, began building Azay-le-Rideau in 1518. Since he had to flee in 1527, it is possible that the residence was never completed—it is thought that it might have been intended to consist of four buildings in all. A tower, dating from feudal times and still visible in this lithograph, was demolished in 1845, being replaced by a small tower in the same style as the rest of the château.

Azay-le-Rideau, Seen from the Banks of the Indre.

The main building, part of which stands on piles, is mirrored in the waters of the River Indre (*page 109*). On the photo above the purely decorative function of the towers is particularly evident.

Azay-le-Rideau: Interior Decoration.

The interior of the château has been decorated with period furniture from the reserve collection of the musée de Cluny. On the first floor, in the red room (*on left*), hung with red damask from the château d'Effiat (Puy-de-Dôme), there is an 18th century cabinet, on which stand dishes belonging to the school of Bernard Palissy.

Above: stone bust, Renaissance period, of a woman in provincial style head-dress.

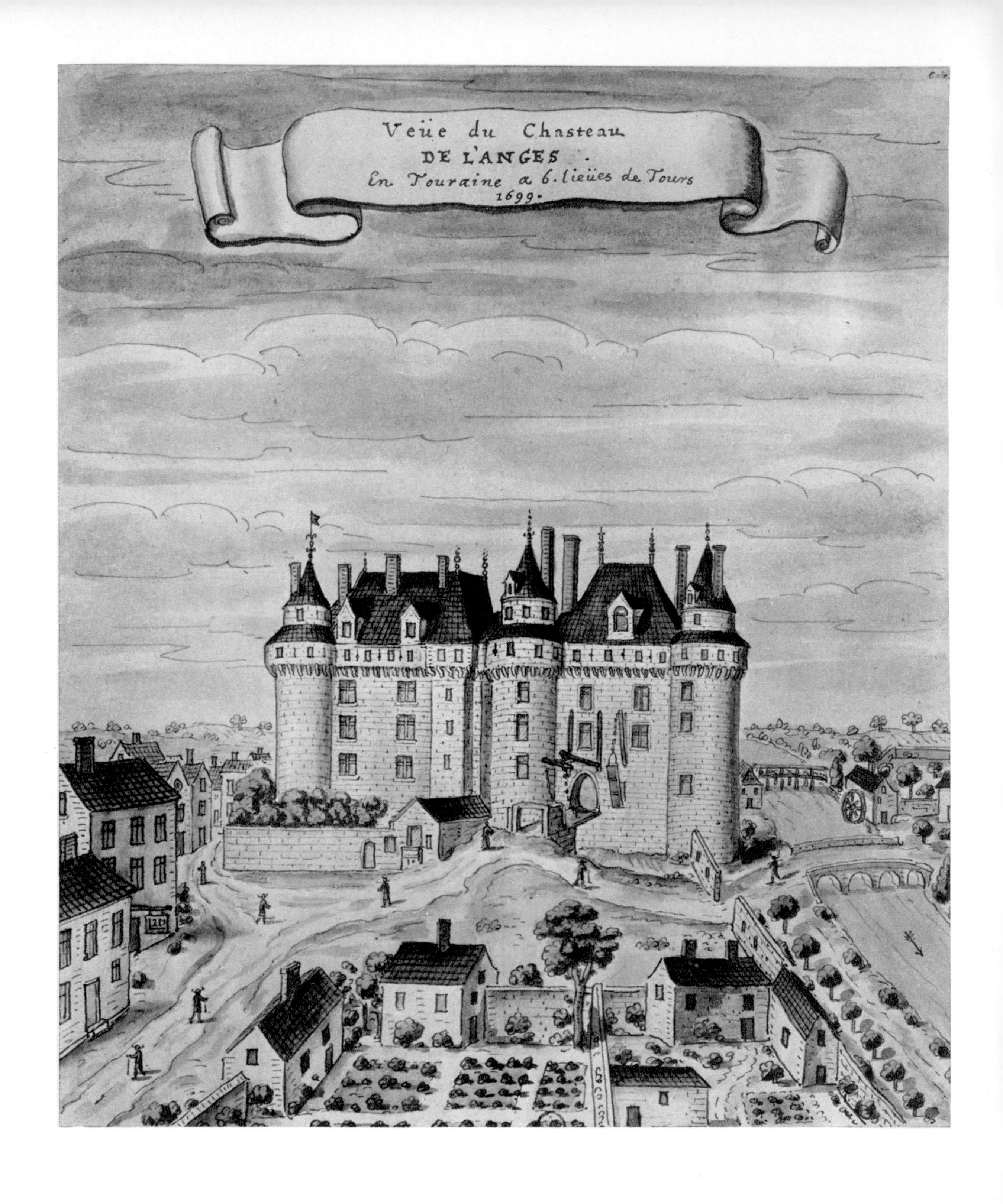

Langeais in the 17th Century (Aquarelle from the Gaignières Collection, Bibliothèque Nationale).

A comparison of this drawing with the château as it looks today shows that the edifice has scarcely changed with the centuries. This martial façade contrasts sharply with the garden front (*pages 114-115*), which is more friendly of aspect and accessible.

Langeais, Seen from the Village.

Although the ramparts have been pierced by large windows, admittedly rather far off the ground, the defensive potential of the château is not negligible: notice the continuous round way, dominated by another storey lying further back.

The interior was completely furnished at the end of the last century by Jacques Siegfried. It contains a pair of portraits, painted on wood, of Charles VIII and Anne de Bretagne (French School, late 15th century) hung in the room where their marriage contract was signed (*see pages 118-119*).

Ussé.

The château was built in various stages during the second half of the 15th century. These stages are discernible in the photograph above. In chronological order and from right to left, they are: the south wing, oldest of all, but remodelled during the 18th century; then the beginning of the east wing, erected a few years later; the continuation of this wing, and then the north wing, definitely the most recent, a large part of which was demolished during the 17th century to open up the view on to the Loire. The influence of Langeais is clearly visible in this last section of the building.

The chapel, built between 1520 and 1538, has been adorned with beautiful Aubusson tapestries, featuring human figures. On right: a late 17th century work depicting an episode in the *Histoire d'Alexandre.*

The general view of the château on pages 122-123 shows the east front, which has remained almost intact, the west front, rebuilt in the 16th century, the north-west tower, which doubtless marked the completion of the original building, about the year 1480, and the pavilion erected during the reign of Louis XIV.

Chinon.

The château of Chinon rises up on a promontory dominating the River Vienne. It is composed of three distinct parts: the du Coudray fort, the du Milieu château and the Saint-Georges fort, which is joined to the foregoing by a bridge watched over by the Clock Tower (tour de l'Horloge), at left. On the roof of this tower a small lantern tower will be seen, housing the *Marie Javelle* bell, which dates back to the 16th century.

The du Milieu section used to contain the royal apartments, all that remains of which is this gable, with a fireplace still hanging from it. It was in this room, on the first floor, that Charles VII received Joan of Arc.

Chinon in the 17th Century (Aquarelle from the Gaignères Collection, Bibliothèque Nationale).

The artist's imagination has grouped the various buildings together and placed them on rectilinear foundations. Nevertheless, by comparing this drawing with the photo of the château as it is today (*see opposite*), one can see that some of the walls have lost their upper sections and some of the towers their roofs.

Chinon, Seen from the Opposite Bank of the Vienne.

From right to left: the Clock Tower (notice its thinness, not obvious in the photo on page 124), the ramparts, the square tower, the ruins of the royal apartments, with, in front, the tour du Trésor, the tour de Boisy, crenelated in the fantastic style of the 19th century, and the du Coudray keep. The entire front seen here is about 300 feet long. The length of this château is reminiscent of some English castles, Windsor, for instance.

Montsoreau in the 17th Century.

Completed in 1455, this château, as can be seen on the drawing reproduced above, stands right on the edge of the river, though today it is separated from it by a road. In the 16th century it was owned by Charles de Chambes, one of the fiercest executioners during the massacre of St. Bartholomew's Day. It was he who assassinated Bussy d'Amboise, though not in this château, as Alexandre Dumas records, but at the château of la Coutancière.

Montsoreau, Façade Facing on to the Courtyard.

Purchased by the Department of Maine-et-Loire, the château has been restored by the department of historical buildings and monuments, which has renovated the roofs. Notice the special arrangement of the dormer-windows opening on to the round way, a formula which was later repeated at Azay-le-Rideau. The two re-entrant angles are provided with octagonal stairway towers. Today the building houses the Moroccan Tribes Museum.

Above: *Boumois.*

This château was constructed during the early years of the 16th century for René de Thory, close to the first château, which was destroyed by the English. The round way, continuous along three sides, and the further, smaller storey added to the towers, in imitation of Langeais, are more for decoration than defence. The windows were enlarged and altered during the 17th century. During the 18th century the château belonged to the Aubert du Petit-Thouars family.

Right: *Boumois, Façade Overlooking the Courtyard.*

Here one sees the living apartments, well restored in recent years on the lines of the original design.

Montreuil-Bellay in the 17th Century (Aquarelle in the Gaignières Collection, Bibliothèque Nationale).

This water-colour does certainly show the collection of buildings which constitute the château of Montreuil-Bellay, even though their arrangement is more or less imaginary. From left to right: the ramparts, the huge collegiate chapel, the 'little château', enclosing an older and smaller castle, and on the right, on the banks of the Thouet, the new château (Château-Neuf), with its large towers crowned with overhanging parapets. The Petit Château is made up of the apartments of the four châtelains, each with its own individual entrance and staircase tower.

Landifer.

This small château, doubled in size about the year 1900, was built during the reign of Charles IX, and the lack of security during the period of the Wars of Religion is marked by the narrowness of the entrance and by the loopholes studding the walls. The work of local masons, this château shows signs of a certain awkwardness, particularly in the distribution and disposition of the bays, and also in the naïvety of the ornamentation, a naïvety not without its charm, however.

Above: *Montgeoffroy.*

Built between 1772 and 1776 by Barré, the architect who built the château du Marais, and rather restrained in style, Montgeoffroy, which has retained the chapel and two entrance towers of a former pre-15th century edifice, has also preserved the decoration and furniture of the time of its construction. It was built for the maréchal de Contades.

Right: *Saumur, General View.*

The line of houses, the quays, the Saint-Pierre belfry and, above all, the quiet waters of the Loire form a beautiful accompaniment to the powerful silhouette of the château as seen in this photograph.

Saumur.

In the château of Saumur, constructed during the 14th century, the former fortress has become a fortified palace. The towers, shelving-off towards the base, are crowned with crenelated round ways with mâchicoulis, but the latter are decorated with clover-leaf designs, purely for effect. Comparison with the miniature in the *Très Riches Heures du duc de Berry* series reveals that various transformations and simplifications took place during the 18th and 19th centuries. Since this photograph was taken, the gateway tower and the tower on the left have been restored.

Saumur.

In recent years the collections of the Museum of Saumur have been put on display in a striking manner, by exhibiting them in the rooms of the château. In this photograph we see above the fireplace a portrait, *en médaillon,* of the Duchess of Maine, with, on the right, a portrait of Lauzun, a relic from the works of Sir Peter Lely. (Below this portrait a number of bookbindings will be noticed, arranged in the book-case. They include one in lace-work, attributed to Derome le Jeune).

Following pages (138-139): *Brissac.*

Brissac.

When, in 1606, Charles de Cossé, Marshal of France, had Jacques d'Angluze reconstruct his château, the 15th century edifice was gradually demolished as the new building progressed, but this process was brusquely interrupted in 1621, resulting in the paradoxical appearance the château presents to the world today. This is obvious in the photograph above and that on pages 138-139. D'Angluze's first plan was to demolish the right-hand tower, to complete the wing already begun and then to rebuild the tower.

Left: the Mortemart bedroom.

Angers.

Pages 142-143: In the centre of the fortifications one sees the chapel, with the royal apartments behind it, adjoining the little castle, on the left of which is the modern gallery containing the Apocalypse Tapestries.

Above: The towers, composed of courses of sandstone and granite, were reduced during the reign of Henri III to the same level as the linking ramparts.

Other tapestries have been preserved in the royal apartments too. The one above, known as the *Lady at the Organ*, dates from the 15th century. It is an example of the " mille fleurs " type of tapestry and probably came from the château of Verger.

Angers: The Apocalypse (pages 145 and 146).

Commissioned by Duke Louis I of Anjou from the Parisian artist Nicolas Bataille, the Apocalypse series of tapestries (1373-1380) is one of the most celebrated in the world. Sold by the Domains Directorate in 1843, as being objects of no use, the tapestries were bought back by the Bishop of Angers. In 1954 they were returned to the château, where a special building was erected for them by Monsieur Bernard Vitry. Here (*page 145*) we see the ninth item in the series, showing Death arriving on his green horse, with a depiction of hell behind him, and (*page 146*) a detail from the fourth item, representing the old men.

Le Plessis-Bourré.

This Angevin château was built during the reign of Louis XI by Jean Bourré, the Financial Secretary, who had just directed the building operations at Langeais. *Above:* the fortified entrance gateway, with its double drawbridge and ornate mâchicoulis. *Left*: Interior: a 16th century sideboard with an Aubusson tapestry on the wall behind it, bearing a pastoral scene.

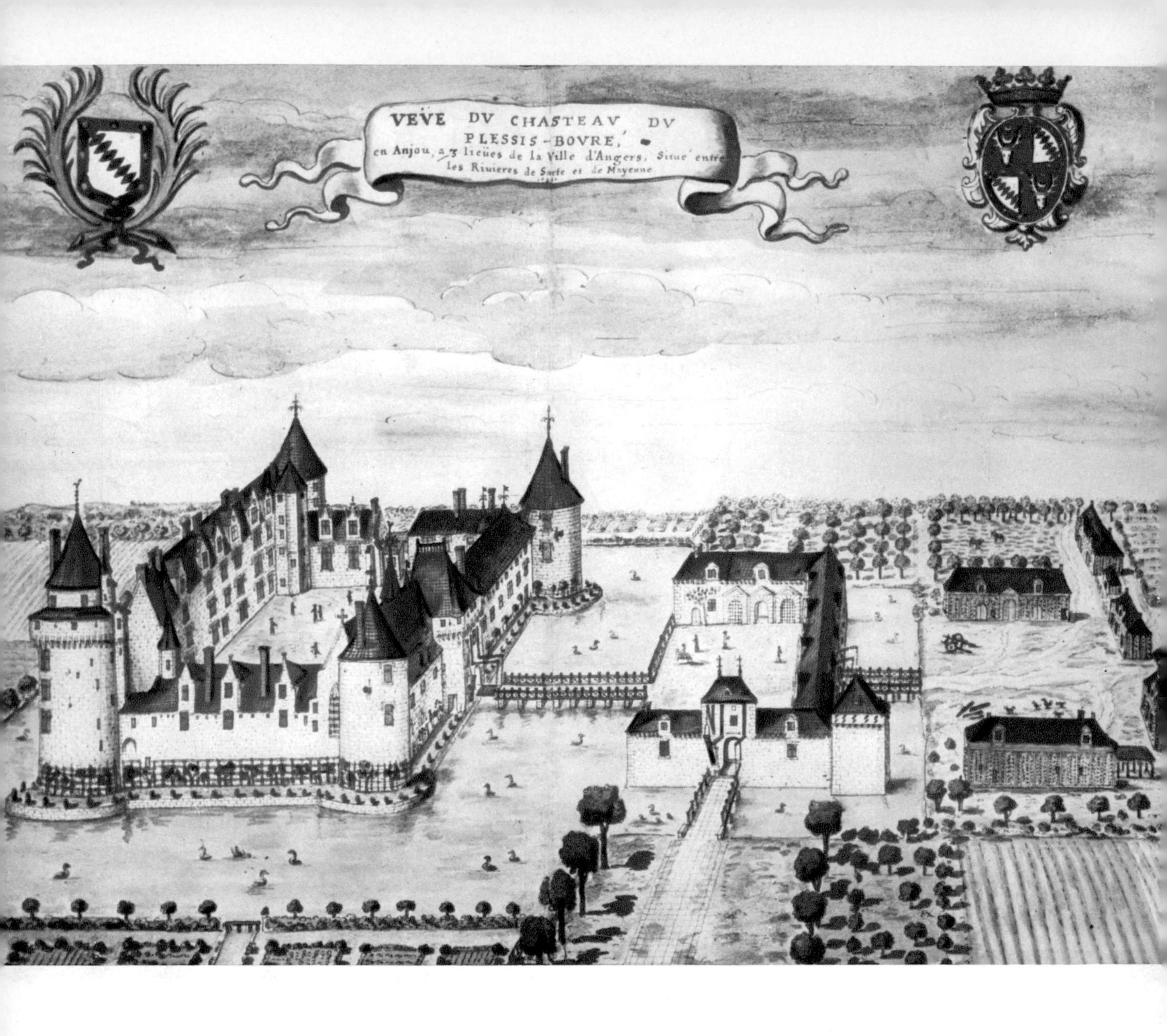

Le Plessis-Bourré in the 17th Century (Aquarelle in the Gaignières Collection, Bibliothèque Nationale).

From right to left we see: the entrance pavilion and adjoining buildings, the stables etc., reconstructed during the 17th century, the seven-arched bridge, over 45 yards long, and finally, the château proper. It is clear from this view that the château's defences relied mainly on the width of the moats, sufficient to obviate any damage from attacking artillery. The only connection between the château and its outbuildings is via bridges equipped with drawbridges.

Le Plessis-Bourré.

This photograph, taken almost from the same angle as the water-colour drawing opposite, shows that the château has remained almost entirely in its original state. It will be noticed that the seigneurial living quarters are at a higher elevation than the rooms in the side wings, in order to give more light and air. The tower on the left has obviously been influenced by the towers of Langeais.

Les Réaux.

This château, originally called " le Plessis-Rideau ", was constructed during the 16th century. The chequered pattern of the brickwork had appeared for the first time at Chatigny in the preceding century, reaching Normandy some years after. The château got its name in the middle of the 17th century from its proprietor, Tallemant des Réaux, author of the *Historiettes*. This postern gate entrance, devoid of any military pretensions, is all that remains of the 16th century château.

On the right: *Nantes*.

Nantes.

The enceinte, enclosed by the towers of the château of the Dukes of Brittany and formerly encircled by the waters of the Loire, was built from 1466 on by Duke François II, according to plans drawn up by Mathurin Rodier.

The entrance gateway (*page 153*) is enclosed by two towers, the tour de la Boulangerie and the tour du Pied-de-Biche. There is an 18th century bridge followed by a 15th century drawbridge. On the tour de la Boulangerie (right) we see the coat of arms of Brittany.

The large Fer-à-Cheval tower projects from the east front of the château (*on left in photograph above*) and is joined to the tour de la Rivière (*in foreground*) by a rampart partially rebuilt by the duc de Mercoeur at the end of the 16th century. Beyond rise the roofs of the main living quarters (Grand-Logis).

Nantes, the Grand-Logis.

Built in the days of Anne de Bretagne, this severe-looking, four-storeyed residence is crowned with richly decorated dormer windows in the flamboyant style and ends on the south side in the *pavillon de la Couronne-d'Or*, containing two parallel staircases, pierced in their upper reaches by loggias.

Nantes, the Well.

This well stands in front of the Grand-Logis. Its octagonal wall is decorated with escutcheons, carved in stone, and surmounted by an elegant wrought-iron structure accommodating no less than seven pulleys.

ARCHITECTURAL FEATURES IN CHRONOLOGICAL ORDER

Langeais, keep: c. 990.
Montrésor, towers: end of 10th century.
Cinq-Mars, tower: 11th century.
Semblançay, keep: 11th century.
Beaugency, keep: end of 11th century.
Loches, keep: end of 11th century.
Cinq-Mars, tower: 12th century.
Villandry, keep: 12th century.
Loches, keep, wall coverings: 12th century.
Le Grand Pressigny, keep: 12th century.
Le Coudray-Montbault, towers: 12th century.
Le Plessis-Macé, old portion: 12th century.
Montbazon, keep: 12th century.
Angers, remnants of Geoffroy le Bel: middle of 12th century.
Montrichard, keep: 12th century.
Chinon, du Moulin tower and base of Clock Tower: 12th century.
Chinon, Saint-Georges Fort: second half of 12th century.
Chinon, l'Echauguette Tower and des Chiens Tower: end of 12th century-beginning of 13th century.
Giens, south tower: end of 12th-beginning of 13th century.
Luynes, enceinte: 12th and 13th century.
Meung, old part: 1206-1221.
Angers, enceinte: 1230 - c. 1241.
La Bussière, old parts: 13th century.
Montpoupon, large tower: 13th century.
Nantes, old keep: 13th century.
La Motte-Sonzay, towers: 13th century.
Blois, Assembly Room: 13th century.
Selles-sur-Cher, feudal château: 13th century.
Chinon, du Coudray Tower: 13th century.
Clisson, east part: 13th century.
Avaray, towers: 13th century.
Montreuil-Bellay, the old château: 13th century.
Sainte-Maure, tower: 14th century.
Chinon, Clock Tower (upper part): 14th century.
Bellegarde, keep: 14th century.
Le Châtellier, keep: 14th century.
Sully, the old château: end of 14th century, perhaps according to Raymond du Temple's plans.
Saumur: end of 14th century.
Le Coudray-Montpensier: end of 14th century-beginning of 15th century.
Loches, royal apartments (old rooms): beginning of 15th century.
Angers, Palatine Chapel and royal apartments: beginning of 15th century.
Chissay: reign of Charles VII.
Trèves, keep: c. 1420-1435.
Montsoreau: completed in 1455.
Clisson, monumental entrance and west portion: 15th century.
Montreuil-Bellay, new château: 15th century.
Argy, keep: 15th century.
Ponts-de-Cé, keep: 15th century.
Launay: 15th century.
Cour-sur-Loire: 15th century.
Argenson (ruins): 15th century.
Le Rivau: 15th century.
Bagneaux, fort: 15th century.
Bauge, middle of 15th century.
Vaujours: 15th century.
Coulaine: 15th century.
Chenonceaux, keep: 15th century.
Chatigny: 15th century.
Beaugency, château de Dunois: middle of 15th century.
Le Coudray-Montbault, apartments: 15th century.
Nantes, enceinte: from c. 1466, according to plans of Mathieu Rodier.
Le Plessis-Bourré: 1468-1472.
Langeais. 1455-1470.
Plessis-Lez-Tours: c. 1465 - c. 1475.
Chaumont, west tower and d'Amboise tower: reign of Louis XI.
Montrichard, first enceinte (south side): second half of 15th century.
Brissac, towers: second half of 15th century.
Loches: round tower and martelet: second half of 15th century.
Haute-Goulaine, middle section: second half of 15th century.
Ussé: c. 1450-1480.
Le Lude, north wing: 1457 - c. 1500.
Le Verger: c. 1482-completed before 1488.
Fougères-sur-Bièvre: 1470 - c. 1490.
Le Clos-Lucé: commenced in 1477.
Bridoré, fort (ruins): end of 15th century.
Chinon, d'Argenton tower: end of 15th century.
Le Plessis-Macé, recent sections: end of 15th century.
Jallanges: end of 15th century.
Nantes, grand apartments: end of 15th century.
Le Moulin: 1480-1502, by Jacques de Persigny.
Amboise, chapel: c. 1488-1493.
Amboise, des Minimes tower and Heurtault tower: c. 1488-c. 1495.
Amboise, royal apartments: 1491 - c. 1495.
Talcy: end of 15th century.
Azay-le-Ferron, tower: 1496.
Amboise, Louis XII wing (lower part): end of 15th century-beginning of 16th century, by Colin Biart, Louis Amangeart and Guillaume Senault.
Loches, royal apartments (new rooms): end of 15th century.
Chaumont, east and south wings: completed in 1510.
Gien: 1494-1500.
Jarzé: 1500.
Blois, wing known as 'Charles d'Orleans' wing, Louis XII wing and Saint-Calais chapel: 1498 - c. 1503, perhaps by Colin Biart and Jacques Sourdeau.

Montrésor: c. 1494-1510.
Boumois: first quarter of 16th century.
Candé: 1508 (greatly restored during 19th century).
Cheverny, pavillon des communs: 1510.
La Possonnière, alterations: 1514-1515.
Montpoupon, postern: 1515.
Bury (remains): between 1514 and 1524.
Blois, François I wing: 1515-1524, possibly by Colin Biart and Jacques Sourdeau, under the supervision of Dominique de Cortone.
Chenonceaux, Thomas Bohier's château: 1515 - c. 1525, perhaps by Pierre Neveu.
Azay-le-Rideau: 1518-c. 1526; architect: Etienne Rousseau.
Le Lude, south wing: 1520-1530.
Sansac: before 1529.
Le Gué-Péan: first half of 16th century.
Amboise, Louis XII wing (upper part): reign of François I.
Saint-Aignan: reign of François I.
Nantes, Petit-Gouvernement: reign of François I.
Azay-le-Ferron, François I pavilion: reign of François I.
Champigny-sur-Veude, Sainte-Chapelle: 1508-1588.
L'Islette: 1526-1531.
Ussé, chapel: 1520-1538.
La Cote: c. 1529.
Villandry: c. 1532 - c. 1536.
Chambord, main apartments: 1519 - c. 1546, by Dominique de Cortone, Jacques et Denis Sourdeau, Pierre Neveu and Jacques Cocqueau, possibly on the basis of certain designs by Leonardo da Vinci.
Villesavin: c. 1537.
Valençay: west wing: 1540 - c. 1550 perhaps to plains by Philibert Delorme.
Poncé-sur-le-Loir: c. 1542.
Montgeoffroy, chapel: from 1543 onwards.
Serrant, north part: 1546, to designs by Philibert Delorme.
Le Rivau, stables: 16th century.
Le Châtellier, seignorial apartments: 16th century.
Brézé: 16th century.
Herbault: 16th century.
Noizay, wings: 16th century.
Le Grand-Pressigny, new château: c. 1550.
Chenonceaux, des Dômes building, c. 1550, perhaps by Philibert Delorme.
Clisson, south works: 16th century.
Saché: 16th century.
La Motte-Sonzay, courtyard fronts: 16th century.
Les Réaux, postern and chapel: 16th century.
Villegongis: 1530 - c. 1575, by Pierre Neveu.
Marcilly-sur-Maulne: reign of Henry II.
Beauregard, main apartments: c. 1545 - c. 1553, perhaps to plans by Philibert Delorme.
Chenonceaux, bridge: 1555-1559, certainly by Philibert Delorme.
Cheverny, outhouses courtyard: between 1551 and 1565, perhaps under the supervision of Philibert Delorme.
Chambord, enceinte: c. 1546 - c. 1570.
Valençay, keep: c. 1560.
Le Grand-Pressigny, grotto: c. 1560.
Landifer: second half of 16th century.
Angers, governors' apartments: second half of 16th century.
Chenonceaux, gallery: c. 1580, by Denis Courtin.
Cerelles, château de Baudry: reign of Henri III.
Sully, small château: end of 16th century.
Nantes, 'Cavalier-Saint-Pierre' bastion: 1582-1592.
Château-Renard, château de la Motte: beginning of 17th century.
Selles-sur-Cher, large château: 1604 - c. 1630.
Sully, Bêthune tower: after 1602.
Azay-le-Rideau, chapel: 1603.
Haute Goulaine, wings: beginning of 16th century.
Brissac, body of main apartments: 1610-1621, by Corbineau and Jacques d'Angluze.
Cheverny: 1625-1634, by Jacques Bougier.
La Source: 1632.
Beauregard, wing and 'return': 1631-1638.
Richelieu: 1631-1639, by Jacques Lemercier.
Serrant, south section: 1636.
La Roche-Racan: c. 1636.
Blois, Gaston d'Orléans wing: c. 1635-1638, by François Mansard.
Azay-le-Ferron, Humières wing: 1638.
La Ferté-Saint-Aubin: 1635-1650, to designs by François Mansard.
Menars, central section: c. 1645.
Le Plessis-Bourré, outhouses: 17th century.
Valençay, south wing: c. 1650.
Luynes, south wing pavilions: c. 1650, by Le Muet.
Noizay, central section: 1653.
Nantes, Grand-Gouvernement: second half of 17th century.
Azay-le-Rideau, outhouses: second half of 17th century.
Serrant, chapel: second half of 17th century, by J. Hardouin Mansard.
Ussé, west pavilion: second half of 17th century.
Châteauneuf-sur-Loire, pavilion: end of 17th century.
Azay-le-Ferron, Breteuil pavilion: completed in 1714.
Bellegarde, Antin pavilion: 1717.
Bellegarde, other pavilions: beginning of 18th century, by Robert de Cotte.
La Ferté-Saint-Aubin, outhouses pavilions: first half of 18th century.
Valençay, Neuve tower: 18th century.
Veretz, tower: 18th century.
Meung, Jarente wing and chapel: 18th century.
Avaray: 18th century.
Basses-Rivières: 18th century.
Azay-sur-Cher, château de Leugny: 18th century, by André Portier.
Ménars, wing and courtyard buildings: c. 1760 - c. 1764, by A. J. Gabriel.
Ménars, courtyard gallery, orangery and workshops: 1764-c. 1768, by Soufflot.
Montgeoffroy: 1772-1776, by Barré.
Chanteloup, entrance pavilions: Louis XVI period.
Le Lude, east wing: Louis XVI period, by Barré.
Pignerolle: end of 18th century, by Bardoult de La Bigottière.
Nantes, harness store: 1784.
Rochecotte, parts of the buildings: early 19th century.
Les Hayes: 1800-1835.
Challian-la-Poterie: early 19th century.
La Grenadière: early 19th century.
Azay-le-Rideau, courtyard tower: 1845.
La Jumellière: second half of 19th century.
La Turmelière: second half of 19th century.
Champtoceaux: second half of 19th century.
Pontchevron: early 20th century.
Angers, tapestry gallery: 1952, by Bernard Vitry.

BIBLIOGRAPHY (Works of General Reference)

André Hallays, *En flânant à travers la France, Touraine, Anjou et Maine* (Paris, 1918).

Charles Terrasse, *l'Art des châteaux de la Loire* (Paris, 1927).

Louis Hautecoeur, *Histoire de l'architecture classique en France* (Paris, from 1943).

J. Martin-Demézil, *le Loir-et-Cher* (Paris, 1946).

F. Lesueur, *Blois, Chambord et les châteaux du Blésois* (Paris, 1947).

J. M. Rougé, *Au pays merveilleux des châteaux de Touraine.*

Pierre Leveel, J.-M. Rougé, Emile Dacier et Jacques Guignard, *Visages de la Touraine* (Paris, 1948).

Ernest de Ganay, *Châteaux de France, région de l'Ouest* (Paris, 1949).

R. Ranjard, *la Touraine archéologique* (Tours, 1949).

Henry de Ségogne, *Eure-et-Loir, Loir-et-Cher, Indre-et-Loire, Maine-et-Loire* (Paris, 1950).

André Castelot, *les Grandes Heures des cités et châteaux de la Loire* (Paris, 1953).

Régine Pernoud, *Dans les pas de Jeanne d'Arc* (Paris, 1956).

Roland de La Moussaye, *Petit Guide des châteaux et palais de la Loire* (Paris, 1956).

François Gébelin, *les Châteaux de la Loire* (Paris, 1957).

Jean Morin, Jacques Levron, Henri Enguehard, *le Maine-et-Loire* (Paris, 1957).

Raymond Ritter, *Châteaux, donjons et places fortes* (Paris, 1958).

Georges Monmarché and Charles Bacquet, *Val de Loire* (« Guides bleus », Paris, 1958).

Jacques Levron, *Châteaux et vallée de la Loire* (Paris, 1958).

Parcs et châteaux de France (Paris, Commissariat général au tourisme, 1960).

Pierre du Colombier, *le Château de France* (Paris, 1960).

Société française d'archéologie: congrès archéologique d'Orléans, 1892, d'Angers et Saumur, 1910, de Blois, 1925, d'Orléans, 1930, de Tours, 1947.

INDEX

NOTES

The châteaux of Chambord, Chaumont, Azay-le-Rideau, Angers, Talcy and Fougères-sur-Bièvre belong to the State and are administered by the Service des Monuments historiques; the Richelieu estate is the property of the University of Paris; the château of Langeais that of the Institut de France; the châteaux of Loches, Chinon, Le Grand-Pressigny (Museum of Prehistory), Saché (Balzac Museum), belong to the Department of Indre-et-Loire; Montsoreau (Goums Museum) belongs to the Department of Maine-et-Loire; Gien (Museum of the Hunt and of Falconry), la Bussière (Museum of Angling), Beaugency (Dunois Museum), Sully-sur-Loire and Châteauneuf belong to the Department of Loiret; Montrichard, Blois (museums and library), Bellegarde (town hall), Saumur (Museum of the Decorative Arts and Equestrian Museum), Nantes (Museum of the Decorative Arts, Breton Museum and Navy Museum), Ponts-de-Cé, Baugé (town hall), Durtal (asylum) and the keeps of Meung and Trèves, belong to their respective towns; the châteaux of Plessis-lez-Tours (municipality of La Riche), Basses-Rivières (municipality of Rochecorbon, Vine and Wines of Touraine Museum) and Azay-le-Ferron (department of Indre) belong to the town of Tours; the ruins of the château of Vaujours belong to the town of Château-la-Vallière; the châteaux of Amboise (His Royal Highness, the Comte de Paris), of Montrésor (the comtesse E. Rey), Cinq-Mars (Monsieur Untersteller), of Villandry (Monsieur François Carvallo), of Montreuil-Bellay (Baron de Grandmaison), of Chenonceaux (Monsieur Menier), of Le Plessis-Bourré (Monsieur Reille-Soult, duc de Dalmatie), of Ussé (comte Louis de Blacas), of Le Lude (Monsieur de Talhouet), of le Clos-Lucé (Leonardo da Vinci Museum —comte Saint-Bris), of Le Moulin (Monsieur de Marchéville), of Brissac (duc de Brissac), of Boumois (Monsieur Grillault Laroche) of Cheverny (marquis de Vibraye), of Beauregard (Mme de Gosselin), of Villesavin (comte and comtesse Erik de Sparre), of Marcilly-sur-Maulne (baronne de Champchevrier), of Serrant (duchesse de la Trémoille), of Montbazon (Miss Liliane Witteker), of Montgeoffroy (marquis de Contades), of Valençay (duchesse de Valençay), of La Ferté-Saint-Aubin (comte d'Hofflize), of Ménars (Compagnie de Saint-Gobain), of the château de la Source, at Olivet (Mme. Dreux-Boucart), of the two châteaux of Selles-sur-Cher (comte d'Ardemare) and the pagoda of Chanteloup (Colonel Faure) are all private property open to the public. The châteaux d'Avaray (jointly owned), of l'Islette (Société civile et immobilière du château de l'Islette), of Landifer (Banque de Paris et des Pays-Bas) and all other châteaux mentioned in this work are private property and are not open to the public.

ACKNOWLEDGMENT FOR PHOTOGRAPHS

ARCHIVES PHOTOGRAPHIQUES, PARIS: 26, 30, 32, 34, 35, 41, 49, 64, 69, 72, 74, 77, 82, 83, 92, 104, 105, 110, 113, 116, 128, 132, 141, 146, 147, 149, 150.

ARSICAUD, TOURS: 80, 81, 95, 99.

BOULAS J., Orléans: 13.

BULLOZ, Paris: 126

EDITIONS D'ART YVON, Paris: 153, 154, 155, 156.

FRANCESCHI: 55.

GIRAUDON, Paris: 29, 44, 46, 47, 84, 85, 86, 87, 98, 120.

ISTITUTO GEOGRAFICO DE AGOSTINI - S. p. A., Novara: 14, 15, 33, 36, 37, 39, 40, 42, 45, 48, 51, 52, 53, 54, 56, 65, 68, 93, 96, 97, 100, 108, 109, 112, 118-119, 121, 125, 137, 144, 145, 148, 151.

JAHAN PIERRE, Paris: 19, 58, 63.

KARQUEL, Aulnay sous-Bois: 21, 28, 38, 43, 59, 60, 62, 102, 103, 122-123, 129, 130, 131, 152.

KNECHT SYLVAIN, Tours: 75, 76, 117.

LAGRAVE ROGER, Paris: 140.

PHOTOTHÈQUE FRANÇAISE, Paris: jacket, 16, 18, 20, 24, 57, 70-71, 78-79, 133, 134, 138-139, 142-143.

RENÉ-JACQUES, Paris: 22-23, 25, 31, 45, 50, 66, 67, 73, 88, 90-91, 101, 114-115, 124, 135, 136.

ROUBIER JEAN, Paris: 111.

VIOLLET, Paris: 17, 27, 61, 89, 94, 106-107, 127.

Printed in Italy by Istituto Geografico De Agostini S.p.A. - Novara - 1968
Imprimé en Italie - Stampato in Italia